# Naked and
# Not Ashamed

BISHOP T.D. JAKES

**Treasure House**
An Imprint of
**Destiny Image® Publishers, Inc.**
**P.O. Box 310**
**Shippensburg, PA 17257-0310**

"For where your treasure is,
there will your heart be also." Matthew 6:21

Woman Thou Art Loosed! Gift Set ISBN 0-7684-3036-4

For Worldwide Distribution
Printed in the U.S.A.

Gift Edition: 2001
First Printing: 2001          Second Printing: 2002

This book and all other Destiny Image, Revival Press, MercyPlace, Fresh Bread, Destiny Image Fiction, and Treasure House books are available at Christian bookstores and distributors worldwide.

For a U.S. bookstore nearest you, call **1-800-722-6774**.
For more information on foreign distributors, call **717-532-3040**.
Or reach us on the Internet:
**www.destinyimage.com**

# DEDICATION

This book is dedicated to all the many people whose trials and traumas have exempted them from sharing their contributions with this world! You may often be intimidated, but you are not isolated. The best kept secret in ministry is that God can do so much with so little. As you find your way out of the shadows and into the light, we await your return. The greatest voice is the one that comes to us from the grave. I pray that God gives you the courage to come out of the grave clothes and go on with your life. I hope this book gives you the greatest gift any one of us has ever known—a second chance!

# CONTENTS

# Chapter 1

## THE FEAR OF THE FATHER

Have you ever tasted that cold, acid-like taste of fear? I mean the kind of fear that feels like a cinder block is being dragged across the pit of your stomach. It's the kind where cold chills trimmed with a prickly sensation flood your body, adorning itself in a distinct sense of nausea. No matter how strong we are, there is always something that can cause the heart to flutter and the pulse to weaken.

Fear is as lethal to us as paralysis of the brain. It makes our thoughts become arthritic and our memory sluggish. It is the kind of feeling that can make a graceful person stumble up the stairs in a crowd. You know what I mean—the thing that makes the articulate stutter and the rhythmic become spastic. Like an oversized growth, fear soon becomes impossible to camouflage. Telltale signs like trembling knees or quivering lips betray fear even in the most disciplined person. Fear is the nightmare of the stage; it haunts the hearts of the timid as well as of the intimidated.

From the football field to the ski slope, fear has a visa or entrance that allows it to access the most discriminating crowd. It is not prejudiced, nor is it socially conscious. It can attack the impoverished or the aristocratic. When it grips the heart of a preacher, his notes turn into a foreign language and his breathing becomes asthmatic.

To me, there is no fear like the fear of the innocent. This is the fear of a child who walks into a dark basement to find the light switch far from reach—and every mop and bucket becomes a sinister, sleazy creature whose cold breath lurks upon the neck of life's little apprentice. I can remember moments as a child when I thought my heart had turned into an African tom-tom that was being beaten by an insane musician whose determined beating would soon break through my chest like the bursting of a flood-engorged dam.

Even now I can only speculate how long it took for fear to give way to normalcy, or for the distant rumble of a racing heart to recede into the steadiness of practical thinking and rationality. I can't estimate time because fear traps time and holds it hostage in a prison of icy anxiety. Eventually, though, like the thawing of icicles on the roof of an aged and sagging house, my heart would gradually melt into a steady and less pronounced beat.

I confess that maturity has chased away many of the ghosts and goblins of my youthful closet of fear. Nevertheless, there are still those occasional moments when reason gives way to the fanciful imagination of the fearful little boy in me, who peeks his head out of my now fully developed frame like a turtle sticks his head out of its shell with caution and precision.

## THE LOVE OF THE FATHER

*My little children, of whom I travail in birth
again until Christ be formed in you.*
Galatians 4:19

Thank God that He understands the hidden part within each of us. He understands the child in us, and He speaks to our blanket-clutching, thumb-sucking infantile need. In spite of our growth, income, education, or notoriety, He still speaks to the childhood issues of the aging heart. This is the ministry that only a Father can give.

Have you ever noticed that you are never a grown-up to the ones who birthed you? They completely disregard the gray hairs, crowfeet, and bulging, blossoming waistlines of abundant life. No matter how many children call you "Dad" or "Mom," to your parents you are still just a child yourself. They seem to think you have slipped into the closet to put on grown-up clothes and are really just playing a game. They must believe that somewhere beneath the receding hairline there is still a child, hiding in the darkness of adulthood. The worst part about it is (keep this quiet), I think they are right!

The Lord looks beyond our facade and sees the trembling places in our lives. He knows our innermost needs. No matter how spiritually mature we try to appear, He is still aware that lurking in the shadows is a discarded candy wrapper from the childish desire we just prayed off last night—the lingering evidence of some little temper or temptation that only the Father can see hiding within His supposedly "all grown-up" little child.

It is He alone whom we must trust to see the very worst in us, yet still think the very best of us. It is simply the love of a Father. It is the unfailing love of a Father whose son should have been old enough to receive his inheritance without acting like a child, without wandering off into failure and stumbling down the mine shaft of lasciviousness. Nevertheless, the Father's love throws a party for the prodigal and prepares a feast for the foolish. Comprehend with childhood faith the love of the Father we have in God!

When the disciples asked Jesus to teach them to pray, the first thing He taught them was to acknowledge the *fatherhood* of God. When we say "Our Father," we acknowledge His fatherhood and declare our sonship. Sonship is the basis for our relationship with Him as it relates to the privilege of belonging to His divine family. Similarly, one of the first words most babies say is "Daddy." So knowing your father helps you understand your own identity as a son or daughter. Greater still is the need to know not only *who* my father is, but *how he feels about me*.

It is not good to deny a child the right to feel his father's love. In divorce cases, some women use the children to punish their ex-husbands. Because of her broken covenant with the child's father, the mother may deny him the right to see his child. This is not good for the child! Every child is curious about his father.

> *Philip saith unto Him, Lord, shew us the*
> *Father, and it sufficeth us.* John 14:8

Philip didn't know who the Father was, but he longed to see Him. I can still remember what it was like to fall asleep watching television and have my father pick up my listless, sleep-ridden frame from the couch and carry me up the stairs to bed. I would wake up to the faint smell of his "Old Spice" cologne and feel his strong arms around me, carrying me as if I weighed nothing at all. I never felt as safe and protected as I did in the arms of my father—that is, until he died and I was forced to seek refuge in the arms of my heavenly Father.

What a relief to learn that God can carry the load even better than my natural father could, and that He will never leave me nor forsake me! Perhaps it was this holy refuge that inspired the hymnist to pen the hymn, "What a fellowship, what a joy divine. Leaning on the everlasting arms" ("Leaning On the Everlasting Arms," Elisha A. Hoffman, 1887).

## FEAR OR RESPECT?

> *And unto man He said, Behold, the fear of the*
> *Lord, that is wisdom; and to depart from evil is*
> *understanding.* Job 28:28

The Hebrew term for "fear" in this verse is *yir'ah*, according to *Strong's Exhaustive Concordance of the*

*Bible.* It means a moral fear, or reverence. So what attitude should we have toward our heavenly Father? The Bible declares that we should have a strong degree of reverence for Him. But a distinction must be made here: there is a great deal of difference between fear and reverence.

The term *reverence* means to respect or revere; but the term *fear* carries with it a certain connotation of terror and intimidation. That kind of fear is not a healthy attitude for a child of God to have about his heavenly Father. The term rendered "fear" in Job 28:28 could be better translated as "respect." Fear will drive man away from God like it drove Adam to hide in the bushes at the sound of the voice of his only Deliverer. Adam said, "I heard Thy voice in the garden, and I was afraid…" (Gen. 3:10). That is not the reaction a loving father wants from his children. I don't want my children to scatter and hide like mice when I approach! I may not always agree with what they have done, but I will always love who they are.

I remember an occasion when some students from the elementary school my sons attended saw me for the first time. Because I stand a good 6-feet, 2-inches tall, and weigh 250-plus pounds, the little children were completely astonished. The other children told my sons, "Look at how big your Dad is! I bet he would just about kill you. Aren't you afraid of him?" My sons quickly responded with glee, "Afraid of him? Naah, he's not mean. He's our Dad!" They were not afraid of my stature because they were secure in our relationship. Does that mean they have never been punished? Of course not! What it does mean is they have never been abused! My love holds my judgment in balance.

As imperfect as I admit I am, if I know how to love my children, what about God? Oh friend, He may not approve of your conduct, but He still loves you! In fact, when you come to understand this fact, it will help you improve your conduct.

> *Or despisest thou the riches of His goodness and forbearance and longsuffering; not knowing that the goodness of God leadeth thee to repentance?* Romans 2:4

If this text is true (and it is), then we must tell of God's goodness to those who need to repent. I believe the Church has *confused conviction with condemnation.* The Holy Spirit convicts us of sin. *Conviction* leads us to a place of deliverance and change. *Condemnation* leads us to the gallows of despair and hopelessness.

Why have we withheld from so many bleeding hearts the good news of the gospel? We have replaced this good news with the rambunctious ramblings of self-righteous rhetoric! I believe that we must assume the ministry of reconciliation and cause men to be reconciled back to their God. There is no healing for the sins of man in the bushes of this world. Regardless of the atrocious behavior we discover when we work with the flawed material of human insufficiency, we must remember that the only antidote is in the presence of the Lord. I am convinced that the very people who need healing the most have been driven away from the only Healer they will ever find in this world.

# *Chapter 2*

## No Secrets in the Secret Place

There is no tiptoeing around the presence of God with pristine daintiness—as if we could tiptoe softly enough not to awaken a God who never sleeps nor slumbers. We shuffle in His presence like children who were instructed not to disturb their Father, although God isn't sleepy and He doesn't have to go to work. He is alive and awake, and He is well. We blare like trumpets announcing our successes, but we whisper our failures through parched lips in the shadows of our relationship with Him. We dare not air our inconsistencies with arrogance because we know we are so underdeveloped and dependent upon Him for everything we need.

His holiness is our objective; we have aspired to acquire it for years, but none have attained it. Surely there is some qualitative relationship that we imperfect sons can master in the presence of our Holy Father! I, for one, need a Father whose wrinkled-up eyes can see beyond my broken places and know the longing of my heart.

## NOWHERE TO HIDE

It is the nature of a fallen man to hide from God. If you will remember, Adam also hid from God. How ridiculous it is for us to think that we can hide from Him! His intelligence supercedes our frail ability to be deceptive. Adam confessed (after he was cornered by his Father), "I heard Thy voice in the garden, and I was afraid, because I was naked; and I hid myself" (Gen. 3:10). Do you see what the first man did? He hid himself. No wonder we are lost. We have hidden ourselves. We didn't hide our work or our gifts; we have hidden ourselves.

When a man hides himself from God, he loses himself. What good is it to know where everything else is, if we cannot find ourselves? Our loss causes a desperation that produces sin and separation. Like the prodigal son in chapter 15 of Luke, in our desperation we need to come to ourselves and come out from under the bushes where we have hidden ourselves. We need to become transparent in the presence of the Lord.

Adam's meager attempt at morality caused him to sew together a few leaves in a figgy little apron that was dying even while he was sewing it. Why would a lost man cover himself with leaves? Adam said, "I was afraid." Fear separated this son from his Father; fear caused him to conspire to deceive his only Solution. This fear was not reverence. It was desperation.

If Adam had only run *toward* instead of *away* from God, he could have been delivered! Why then do we continue to present a *God who cannot be approached* to a dying world? Many in the Christian family are still uncomfortable with their heavenly Father. Some Christians do not feel accepted in the beloved. They feel that their relationship with God is meritorious, but they are intimidated because of His holiness. I admit that His holiness all the more exposes our flawed, soiled personhood. Yet His grace allows us to approach Him—though we are not worthy—through the bloody skins soaked with Christ's blood.

We are properly draped and dressed to come into the presence of a Holy God only because His accepted Son, Jesus Christ, has wrapped us in His own identity. Like Adam, we are draped by a bloody sacrifice that has made it possible for us to approach our Father and live.

> *Neither is there any creature that is not manifest in His sight: but all things are naked and opened unto the eyes of Him with whom we have to do.* Hebrews 4:13

It is futile to hide from our Father. It is His intelligence (often referred to as His omniscience) that exposes us! We cannot alter His ability to see, so we need to develop enough security to be comfortable with His intelligence. Who else knows you like God does? If you hide from His perfect love, you will never be able to enjoy a relationship with your heavenly Father and be comfortable enough to sit in His lap.

Peter said, "To whom shall we go?" (Jn. 6:68) The truth is that we have no one else to turn to; yet for some reason, we don't seem to know how to come to Him. We don't realize that we can be accepted by Him and find tender mercy and healing for the scars of life and for our bruised hearts—until our desperation and separation cause us to seek shelter in the presence of the Lord.

## IT TAKES TRUST

> *He that dwelleth in the secret place of the most*
> *High shall abide under the shadow of the*
> *Almighty. I will say of the Lord, He is my*
> *refuge and my fortress: my God; in Him will I*
> *trust.* Psalm 91:1-2

The basis of any relationship must be trust. Trusting God with your successes isn't really a challenge. The real test of trust is to be able to share your secrets, your inner failures and fears. A mutual enhancement comes into a relationship where there is intimacy based on honesty.

Jesus told the woman at the well, a woman whose flaws and failures He had supernaturally revealed, "...true worshippers shall worship the Father in spirit and in truth: for the Father seeketh such [real people, flawed people like the woman at the well] to worship Him. God is a Spirit: and they that worship Him must worship Him in spirit and in truth" (Jn. 4:23-24).

We have nothing to fear, for our honesty with the Father doesn't reveal anything to Him that He doesn't already know! His intellect is so keen that He doesn't have to wait for you to make a mistake. He knows of your failure before you fail. His knowledge is all-inclusive, spanning the gaps between times and incidents. He knows our thoughts even as we unconsciously gather them together to make sense in our own mind!

> *The Lord knoweth the thoughts of man, that they are vanity.* Psalm 94:11

Once we know this, all our attempts at silence and secrecy seem juvenile and ridiculous. He is "the all-seeing One," and He knows perfectly and completely what is in man. When we pray, and more importantly, when we commune with God, we must have the kind of confidence and assurance that neither requires nor allows deceit. Although my Father abhors my sin, He loves me. His love is incomprehensible, primarily because there is nothing with which we can compare it! What we must do is accept the riches of His grace and stand in the shade of His loving arms.

We are balanced by our awareness of *His holiness*, which would condemn us, and of *His love*, which esteems and redeems us. He is far too holy for me to develop arrogance about my humanity, yet He is far too loving for me to be frightened by the emotional dysfunction that comes from being raised by a father whom we can never seem to please!

## God Understands Us

What creates a feeling of wholeness in the heart of the believer is the awareness that while God's standards do not change, neither does His compassion. One thing we search for at every level of our relationships is "to be understood." When I am properly understood, I don't always have to express and explain. *Thank You, Lord, for not asking me to explain what I oft can scarcely express!*

We quickly grow weary when we are around anyone who demands that we constantly qualify our statements and explain our intent. We want to be near those who comprehend the subtle expressions of affection, intimacy, and need—a touch, a brief hug, a sigh emitted in the stillness of a moment. Communication cannot be typed or taught; it must be understood. At this level there is a communication so intense that those who understand it can clearly speak it, even through closed lips. As with lovers staring at each other across a crowded and smoke-filled room, words seem so unnecessary when there is understanding. It is with this kind of understanding that God clearly perceives and understands our every need.

## OPEN COMMUNICATION

I believe that when the Scriptures declare that men "ought always to pray, and not to faint" (Lk. 18:1b), that they are speaking of living in a state of open communication with God, not necessarily jabbering at Him nonstop for hours. Many people say, "I am going to pray for a certain amount of time." They ramble on in prayer for hours on their knees, and they end up watching the clock while they utter mindless rhetoric, trying to get in the specified amount of time in prayer.

Let me ask you, would you want someone to talk to you like that? True friends can drive down a road and lapse in and out of conversation, deeply enjoying each other's company—all without any obligation to maintain a steady rhythm of rhetoric. Their communication is just an awareness of the presence of someone they know and understand. We don't need to labor to create what is already there. I am glad my Savior knows what my speech and my silence suggest. I need not labor to create what we already share in the secret place of our hearts!

What is required of us? We are called to live in a state of openhearted communication with the Lord. Yes, we feel vulnerable when we realize that our hearts are completely exposed before God. Yet every one of us desperately needs to have *someone* who is able to help us, *someone* who is able to understand the issues that are etched on the tablets of our heart!

## Naked Before God

Since we already feel exposed when we realize that there is not one thought we have entertained that God has not seen and heard, then *there is no need for a sanctimonious misrepresentation of who we are*! We no longer need to live under the strain of continual camouflage. Neither flagrant nor flamboyant, we are *naked before Him* in the same sense that a man sprawls naked on the operating table before a surgeon. The man is neither boastful nor embarrassed, for he understands that his exposed condition is a necessity of their relationship. Whether the doctor finds good or evil, what is there is there, and the man's comfort lies in the conviction that the surgeon possesses the wherewithal to restore order to any area that may be in disarray.

> *Blessed are the pure in heart: for they shall see*
> *God.* Matthew 5:8

The purity that attracts the presence of God comes from allowing Him to perpetually flush away the corrosion that threatens to block the abundant arterial flow of His grace and mercy toward us. In short, we need to show Him what is clogging or hindering His flow of life to us so He can clean us and keep us acceptable before Him in love.

The Greek word *katheros* is used here to express "purity." It is from this word that we have the English derivative "catharize," which describes medical processes used to cleanse, flush, or release fluids from the body. God is continually sending a deluge of His cleansing grace into the hearts of His children, *but He can't clean or purify what we hide in the secret corners of our hearts and minds.* The hymnist wrote a powerful verse when he penned:

> *"Lord Jesus, I long to be perfectly whole.*
> *I want Thee forever to live in my soul.*
> *Break down every idol, cast out every foe.*
> *Now wash me and I shall be whiter than snow"*
> ("Whiter Than Snow," James Nicholson, 1872).

I can still remember the great joy that flooded my soul when Christ came into my heart. I was walking on air for weeks. It was, and in fact, still is exciting to me to know that my many deplorable sins have been rinsed from my records by the efficacious blood of the Lamb! I shouted and praised the Lord with an abandonment as if it were the last time I would have to praise the Lord.

Upon reflection, I came to understand that the slate had been cleansed at Calvary, but the *mind* is being renewed from day to day. As images came from time to time with flashbacks of things that haunted the attic of my mind like ghosts unexorcised, I began to seek the Lord *who saved me* for *the grace to keep me*. It was then that I began to realize the great truth that the blood of Christ doesn't just reach backwards into the bleakness of my past debauchery—it also has the power to cover my ongoing struggles!

I hadn't known then that Jesus paid it all! The blood of Christ covers my past, present, and future struggles, not so I could run through my inheritance like the prodigal son (if that were possible), but so I might have a comfort as I lie on the table of His grace. I must relax in this comfort and assurance and allow the tools of day-to-day tests and struggles to skillfully implant into my heart and mind a clearer reflection of His divine nature in me.

## Contented in His Presence

Now, amidst the joy that I still possess, I have a growing appreciation for the peace that comes from knowing I am His child. I am His—even when I feel like a mess, even when I am embarrassed to openly discuss my frailties and flaws, for *His grace is sufficient for me*. I thank Him for the peace He has given to every believer who matures into a trust-filled relationship with Jesus Christ. My initial surgery may be completed, but daily I

17

remain under His intensive care as He monitors my pro-gressions and occasional digressions. I wouldn't trust my future with anybody but Him. What about you?

Dear friend, you will never worship God correctly if you live in the shadows, wrestling with unconfessed sin. Whatever you do, there is an ever-increasing need for you to find a *place of comfort* in the presence of the Lord. It is possible to escape my presence, but not His. He is ever present, waiting on you to stand before Him and be healed.

Open relationships with other people can never be attained until you first drop the towel and stand naked before God. If you cannot trust Him, then all hope is lost. When Mary, the sinner, came and washed Jesus' feet with her tears, some mocked Jesus and discredited Him, insin-uating that He lacked the discernment to know she was a woman with a questionable past (see Lk. 7:39). The sad truth is they had been with Jesus and still didn't know His heart. They had heard His commandments but not His heart. It wasn't that Jesus didn't know the hands that washed His feet had done wrong. It wasn't that He didn't know the hair that dried Him had been let down before. It was that He didn't care!

# *Chapter 3*

## SUPERMAN IS DEAD

The best parts of school when I was an eight-year-old were recess and the walk home from school. I liked recess because it gave me an opportunity to stretch my legs and play with my friends. I liked the walk home from school because I usually had a quarter buried deep within my pocket, hidden somewhere beneath the bubble gum, the baseball cards, and all the other paraphernalia that eight-year-olds think are valuable.

I would save that quarter until we walked down Troy Road toward "old man Harless' " store. Now, that was what we called him if we were sure he wasn't around. But if we saw him, he immediately became "Mr. Harless," complete with "Yes, sir," and "No, sir," and all the other polite things we were instructed to say lest the seats of our pants perish in the fires of my mother's wrath!

That quarter of mine was saved for the brightly colored books that were stacked in a display for all the children to see. There were all of my old friends...Superman and Captain Marvel, Captain America and Spiderman. I would purchase a copy of the latest issue and hurry a little farther down Troy Road. Once I found the old path that led up the hill behind the house, I would start my ascent to the big rock beneath the apple tree. There, hidden from public scrutiny, I would pull out my prized hero magazine and imagine that I was one of these men, a super hero who could transform as needed into anything necessary to destroy the villain.

I know all of this sounds terribly old-fashioned. Maybe it sounds a little too much like a scene that should include Andy Griffith, Aunt Bea, and the whole Mayberry clan, but that was really how it was in the days before children started carrying guns instead of comic books. I grew up reading about heroes. We believed in possibility, and though we were neither wealthy nor affluent, we could escape like a bird through the window of a full-color magazine and become anybody we wanted to be for at least 30 minutes—before my mother's voice would be heard from the rickety back porch behind the house.

## WHERE DID THE HEROES GO?

We need heroes today. We need someone to believe in and look up to. We need someone who has accomplished something to give us the courage to believe in the invisible and feel the intangible. We need role models and men whose shadows we may stand in, men who provide a cool refreshing place of safety away from the despair of our oppressive society. It's just that all the "supermen" in the Church seem to have somehow gotten zapped by "kryptonite." Either they or their reputations have wilted into the abyss of human failure.

What are we going to do as we face this generation? From drug-using political officials to prostitute-purchasing preachers, the stars are falling on the heads of this generation! All of their wonder and dreams have turned into a comic book—a comic book that somehow doesn't seem funny anymore. Where did the heroes go?

This isn't just a church issue. We're suffering from an eroding sense of family, not just of family values. The entire concept of the family, period, has been crumbling because of this society's growing acceptance of non-traditional families. More and more women have chosen to be mothers without choosing fathers, while others have become single parents by necessity, not by choice. The gay community has added to the confusion by establishing "homes" that do not reflect God's original plan for child-rearing. So now we have twisted homes that are producing twisted children.

There is a cry coming up out of the city streets:

*Our fathers went out for coffee and came back with cocaine. Their hands will not tuck us in because their feet are shackled to the prison floor.*

*Mother is out of milk and brother just joined a gang. Even in the neighborhood we used to drive through and dream that we lived in, we see ambulances.*

*Moving vans just moved Mommy away from Daddy, and now we see them by appointment. The whole country has fallen into the trash can like discarded comic books whose story lines are out-of-date. Where are the heroes?*

## HONESTY BEFORE GOD

Our healing will require more than a processional of religious ideas that are neither potent nor relevant. We need to understand that God is able to repair the broken places, but it requires us to expose where those broken places are. If we don't say to Him, "This is where I am hurting," then how can He pour in the oil and the wine?

We need to lay ourselves before Him and seek His face in the beauty of holiness—the holiness that produces wholeness. This isn't a matter of one denomination arguing with another over who is right; it is a matter of a broken family seeking healing and answers that can only come from the presence of God. *I am convinced He can heal whatever we can confess!*

> *Come, and let us return unto the Lord: for He hath torn, and He will heal us; He hath smitten, and He will bind us up.* Hosea 6:1

It is in these moments that we are forced to reevaluate our concepts. Have we misaligned ourselves with God, or were our goals "out of kilter" to begin with? I really believe that we have made the unfortunate error of Old Testament Israel, whose attempt to attain righteousness produced a self-righteous mentality in many.

The Old Testament expressed the righteousness of God, a righteousness that the New Testament fully revealed in the gospel of Jesus Christ. Although the Old Testament could not completely reveal the righteousness of God, it certainly introduced a concept of how God defines holiness to humanity and Israel. God knew that the children of Israel would fail in their attempts to achieve the morality contained in the Law. Through their failures, God wanted the Israelites to find the redemption that He had allocated through the blood. Unfortunately, instead of honestly confessing to God the enormity of their failure, they became increasingly hypocritical. The whole purpose of the Law was spoiled because the fleshly egos of men would not repent and seek divine assistance for justification.

> *For I am not ashamed of the gospel of Christ: for it is the power of God unto salvation to every one that believeth; to the Jew first, and also to the Greek. For therein is the righteousness of God revealed from faith to faith: as it is written, The just shall live by faith.*
> Romans 1:16-17

It takes great courage to exemplify total honesty with God. We have not even been totally released to admit our insufficiencies with others, and sometimes even with ourselves. How tragic! *When we discover our own limitations, we become eligible to discover the all-sufficiency of God.* Here we stand, like Israel in tainted armor, before the presence of a God whose brilliancy dims the radiant brightness of the sun. Yet there is a method to the madness of our predicament.

God knew who we were when He called us. Perhaps the sharp contrast between the people God uses and the God who uses them is to provide the worshiper with a clear distinction of who is to be worshiped!

## REAL HEROES

It is undeniable that we face faltering visions and visionaries. Let us seek God for His divine purpose. Could it possibly be that God's intent is to establish *believable heroes*?

We need no glaring, gleaming, high-polished people for this day! We need heroes whose tarnished suits cannot hide their open hearts or their need to touch broken lives. The cry is going out for something *believable*—for something that even if not glorious, is at least fathomable.

The stress of trying to impress others with elitist presentations of spiraling spiritual altitudes has produced isolation and intimidation. No wonder our leaders are dying in the pulpit and suffering from an epidemic of heart attacks and strokes! It is hard to take an ordinary man from an ordinary background, saddle him with responsibility and tremendous visibility, and tell him, "You must be god-like."

Writing in all honesty, the greatest of the apostles—the writer of most of the New Testament epistles—confessed that though he aspired to "apprehend," he hadn't attained (see Phil. 3:12). In what area did this apostle fail? The Holy Spirit has granted him some semblance of diplomatic immunity that at least affords him the right

24

of privacy in spite of imperfections. Yet we continually eat a perfect word from his stained hands, a word that converts the soul and challenges the most godly amongst us. I speak, of course, of the apostle Paul himself!

> *Brethren, I count not myself to have apprehended: but this one thing I do, forgetting those things which are behind, and reaching forth unto those things which are before, I press toward the mark for the prize of the high calling of God in Christ Jesus.*
> Philippians 3:13-14

Alas, the call is a high calling. Yet it has been answered by lowly men who had the discernment to see a God high and lifted up. They stood on their toes like children, but still fell short of reaching His splendor. In short, the heroes in the Bible were not perfect, but they were powerful! They were not superhuman, but they were revelatory. Often chastised and corrected, they were still not discarded, for the Lord was with them.

Jesus was forever having to correct His disciples. Their pettiness, their anger and stinginess—these faults often reaffirmed the fact that they were "men of like passions." I, for one, am glad that they were. Their human frailties encourage the rest of us that we too can be used by God in spite of our feeble, crippled, and fragmented attempts at piety and true devotion.

## WHAT MAKES A HERO?

At the risk of tarnishing a record that no one believes anyway, could we reevaluate what a hero really is? Isn't a hero someone who puts himself at risk to help someone else? Is it someone whose unselfish heart allows him to take dangerous risks to accomplish definite results to help someone else? I wonder if some of the men and women whom we say "failed" actually tarnished their records by having the courage to climb high enough to take the risks that others would not be willing to take...in order to help others.

No, let's not glamorize sin. Sin is sin and it stinks in the nostrils of God. But have our noses become more sensitive than God's? Would we, like the others outside the tomb, choose to condemn to an eternal grave the man Lazarus, whose decomposing body had been shut up in a tomb for three days and begun to stink? *Thank God that Jesus didn't let the stink stop Him from saving the man.*

You have to be a hero to even expose yourself to the jealousy and cruelty of being raised up as a leader. Leaders are ostracized by their peers and criticized by their subordinates. They serve valiantly, though they often receive blows from satan and stabs from friends. Through it all, they continue to minister as if all were well.

I pause to lift to the throne every man or woman of God who is under attack by the enemy. Whether it be a financial, spiritual, or moral attack, I pray for you, my silent, alienated, wounded physician. May the medicine you have given to others come to your aid and bless you.

May you recover all that satan desires to destroy in your life! In Jesus' name, Amen!

> *These all died in faith, not having received the promises, but having seen them afar off, and were persuaded of them, and embraced them, and confessed that they were strangers and pilgrims on the earth. For they that say such things declare plainly that they seek a country.*
> Hebrews 11:13-14

It is imperative that our vision be both progressive and regressive. In the forefront of our minds must be a plan that promises bright hopes for the future. I often say that a man cannot die with a twinkle in his eye! There must be a strong sense of destiny lodged firmly in our minds that dispels the despair of past failures. We must live our lives facing the rising sun.

Although heroes don't have to be perfect, I realize they must be people who are resilient enough to survive tragedy and adversity. All of us have experienced the pain of adversity in our warfare, whether it was a physical, emotional, economical, spiritual, or sexual attack. Regardless of which category the attack falls under, they are very personal in nature. Real heroes not only survive the incident, but also overcome the lingering side effects that often come from it.

Why do I say that? If you don't survive, you can't save anyone. No young man in a combat zone can carry his wounded comrade if he himself does not survive. Live long enough to invest the wealth of your experience in the release of some other victim whom satan desires to bind or incapacitate!

> *And truly, if they had been mindful of that*
> *country from whence they came out, they*
> *might have had opportunity to have returned.*
> Hebrews 11:15

The faith of these heroes sets them apart from other men. It is your convictions that cause you to be distinctly different from others whose complacency you can't seem to share. The people referred to in Hebrews 11 were not mindful of where they came from. In other words, their minds were full of where they were going. These valiant heroes were not perfect, but they were convinced that what God had promised He was able to perform. Now if their minds had been full of their origin instead of their destiny, they would have gone back. Be assured that *people always move in the direction of their mind*. Whatever your mind is full of, that is where you eventually move. Thank God for people who can see the invisible, and touch with their faith the intangible promises of God.

## HEROES OF FAITH

> *And what shall I more say? for the time would*
> *fail me to tell of Gedeon, and of Barak, and of*
> *Samson, and of Jephthae; of David also, and*
> *Samuel, and of the prophets: who through faith*
> *subdued kingdoms, wrought righteousness,*
> *obtained promises, stopped the mouths of*
> *lions, quenched the violence of fire, escaped*
> *the edge of the sword, out of weakness were*

*made strong, waxed valiant in fight, turned to
flight the armies of the aliens.*
Hebrews 11:32-34

The Scriptures declare that these heroes were made strong out of weakness. In order to be a real success, *you must be able to be strengthened through struggle.* What we need is a hero who can, as these men did, report back to the world that he escaped. He may have felt weak, he may have cried and suffered, but he still made it. Look at these men mentioned in Hebrews 11:32. Examine their lives. They were not glaring examples of flawless character; yet they epitomized faith toward God. Even though most of them experienced failures and flaws, they would have made the front pages of the newspapers in our day for their heroism. We must be careful when judging the weak moments in their lives. Consider the entirety of their lives and you will see that the dent in their armor didn't affect their performance on the battlefield.

Gideon failed the biblical faith test when he sought a sign. Samson shined on the battlefield but had struggles in the bedroom. This anointed judge of Israel wrestled with more than a failed marriage that he could not seem to regain. He had an insatiable appetite for strange flesh, which led to his demise, yet he still made it to the list of the few, the proud, and the brave.

Oh yes, then there is Jephthah, the illegitimate child who was rejected by his siblings and ostracized by his family. He went to the land of Tob where he became what we would call a gang leader. He gathered together the "vain" fellows, a sampling of social rejects, and became their leader. In spite of his adolescent struggles, and his rash tendency to make wild vows (which cost him the destruction of his daughter's future), he still made it to the roll of the renowned. He made it because he believed God. He lifted himself above his circumstances and fought the enemies without and within!

## CHOSEN BY REJECTION

To me, Jephthah's gang reveals the part of ministry that we are missing: *He built an army out of rejects.* There is something powerful about being a "chosen reject"; chosen by God but rejected by men. There is a focus that evolves in the heart of someone who has been rejected by men. Their rejection creates a feeling of misplacement. Have you ever felt misplaced? Have you ever struggled to fit into some network or order in which it seemed you were not welcomed? It is God's design that causes us to experience rejection, even though it is painful.

When we have been ostracized by someone or something that we wanted to belong to, our streaming tears cannot soften the hard truth. Rejection tastes like bile in our gut. However, the experience can make us bitter, or it can make us better. I choose better. What about you?

I believe this kind of pain causes us to achieve a level of consecration that is out of the reach of people who have never been rejected. Why? Once the reality hits us that God purposely chooses to use misplaced and rejected people, then first and foremost, we experience a sense of warm gratitude that flows through our human hearts like hot syrup. It fills every crack and crevice of our minds, which suggested there was no place of meaning for us. It is in the shadows of these moments that we worship behind the veil, wrapped in His Shekinah Glory, enveloped in the love of the sacrificed Lamb of God, the God *who created a place for the misplaced and chose us for Himself.*

I can't help but wonder if we have forsaken some of God's finest people because they were under attack, people whom God wanted to use to make a tremendous statement in the Body of Christ. These vicarious soldiers would have been so glad to receive a second chance to return to active duty. They could bring to us a voice from the grave. They could express the truth that there is life after death.

Dead circumstances cannot hold down the body of someone who has been chosen! If no one else embraces these bleeding, purple heart soldiers, perhaps they should rally together and find comfort in the commonality of their mutual experience. Thank God for Jephthah, who reminds us of the deep, abiding reality that even if we were thrown into a refuse receptacle by closed minds who decided that our dry bones couldn't live again, God is still in the business of recycling human lives!

I must confess that more than once I have seen His hand pick up the pieces of this broken heart and restore back to service my crushed emotions and murky confidence, while I stood in awe at the fact that God can do so much with so little. Isn't that the gospel? Isn't that the good news we are supposed to preach to the poor souls of broken men? Isn't that where the revival must start—in the trash cans of our churches, in the dumpsters of ministries that have discarded what God regarded, and regarded what God has discarded?

The greatest place to preach isn't in our great meetings with swelling crowds and lofty recognitions. The greatest place to preach is in the trenches, in the foxholes and the hogpens of life. If you want a grateful audience, take your message to the messy places of life and scrape the hog hairs off the prodigal sons of God, who were locked away in the hog pens by the spiritual elite.

It is here in these abominable situations that you will find true worship being born, springing out of the hearts of men who realize the riches of His grace. No worship seminar is needed for someone whose tearstained face has turned from humiliation to inspiration. Their personal degradation has become a living demonstration of the depths of the unfathomable love of God! My friend, this is Davidic worship! This is the praise of David, whose critical brothers and distracted father helped him become the canvas on which God paints the finest picture of worship these weary eyes have ever witnessed!

I won't even take the time to point out the obvious indiscretions of King David. Even his obvious anointing and worship did not exempt him from internal conflict, or from a lethal experience with infidelity that would have made a heathen blush. No, I don't want to glamorize the sins of these supermen of faith, but I just had to discuss the fact that we have thrown away a hundred men like them. I am afraid we have killed our heroes because we were looking for the brightly packaged, cartoon-clad individuals we read about.

It is time for us to redefine and redirect our gaze to find the heroes of God among us. We must not forget that God purposely chooses to use misplaced and rejected people, and He may be looking in our direction.

# *Chapter 4*

## THE POWER OF PASSION

*To whom also He shewed Himself alive after
His passion by many infallible proofs, being
seen of them forty days, and speaking of the
things pertaining to the kingdom of God.*
Acts 1:3

Perhaps it is no coincidence that the Greek word *pathos*, usually translated as "suffer" or "to feel," is used here to describe Christ's crucifixion. What a strange choice of expression for such a hideous occurrence. Yet it alludes to a deeper truth that each of us must face. Although the inference is toward His suffering, look a little deeper beneath the sufferings that He experienced and understand that there was an underlying ecstasy beneath the pain of the cross. The writer of Hebrews alludes to it as he lifts the veil and peeks behind the crisis of the cross and reports the purpose of the cross.

*Looking unto Jesus the author and finisher of
our faith; who for the joy that was set before
Him endured the cross, despising the shame,
and is set down at the right hand of the throne
of God.* Hebrews 12:2

The cliché, "No pain no gain," suggests that gain validates the pain we incur. That is only true for the person
who has opened up and allowed himself to want or need
something bad enough to endure the unpleasantness
attached to attaining his goal. The problem with most
people is that they stand around like dreamers, gazing
into the night at distant stars instead of working in the
day to build a ship to reach the stars. Regardless of how
far away the goal may seem, if there is a real passion for
it, we can accomplish much in His name.

## WE NEED PASSION!

Here lies the reality of fulfillment. There can be no
fulfillment where there is no passion. The passion that
causes us to achieve has to be strong enough to make us
uncomfortable. The discomfort that comes from the desire
must be intense enough to keep the obstacles between
you and the thing you desire from aborting the intensity
of your desire! Simply stated, you must want it bad
enough to survive the process required to attain it. It
doesn't matter whether it is a good marriage, a ministry, a
business, or whatever. There will always be hindrances to
overcome. It is the force of your personal passion to
achieve that gives you the force to break down the wall
between you and the thing you desire.

Jesus, our prime example of success, had a cross between Him and His goal. The cross was not the end; it was the means. He didn't enjoy the means, but He endured it—His passion was for the end. What gave Him the power to endure His means to achieve the end? It was His passion.

The desire that burns and inflames your heart, the desire that is forever in your thoughts, becomes the fuel that enables you to withstand whatever life sends against you. His suffering was for the sins of this world. It was more than groping in the gross darkness of a feverish death. It was the suffering of the passionate!

## THE SUFFERING OF THE PASSIONATE

There is an intense discomfort associated with passion and desire. It is not pleasant; it is, in fact, *suffering*. It is an intense, unquenched desire that gnaws at the fibers of our minds, motivating us to actions of fulfillment. Have you ever noticed that God mightily uses some of the most wretched sinners whom He converted into great ministers? It is because these characters were people who were accustomed to passion and acquisition. They were people who dared to desire. They were people who, although misdirected at one time, possessed such a burning passion that, if bridled and directed, could make them people of great accomplishment.

Oh, thou man or woman of great passion, driven by intense feelings and desire, you often wrestle with your ambitious nature. Hear me and hear me well: You don't want to kill your passion; you just need to redirect it toward a godly vision. That is why satan has desired to have you. He knows that if you ever line up your passion with God's purpose, you will become a spiritual dynamo. Then there will be no stopping you until the flames of your passion are quenched in the streams of your eternal destiny!

Do not resent your passion. Control it, yes, but please don't kill it. Without it, you would be as limp as an over-cooked noodle, your life as bland as hospital food. God created you to be zesty and alive! Even though you may have often misdirected your passions, allow God to recycle your feelings. Retrieve your passions from your dusty religious receptacle and place them in God's recycling program!

I realize that passions create suffering. Many people *cease to desire* just to relieve themselves of the pain and struggle of trying to attain their dreams. They become zombies trapped in an intermediate, lukewarm state of existence that is neither hot nor cold! Their lukewarm, placid philosophy causes them to sink into the abyss of mediocrity. They live, marry, buy cars, accumulate stocks, have children, and do everything that their living counterpart does—but without passion, they just basically *go through the motions!*

How sad it is to see them rise out of bed every morning, arms extended, humming a monotone melody of melancholy undertones. They grunt incoherent answers at others as though they are deeply medicated. These mummies may be mommies or daddies; they may even be preachers or teachers. *They are corpses who aren't quite dead*. Their nebulous state of affairs exempts them from pain, but denies them pleasure. Now they are safe from failure, but threatened by depression.

## WAKE UP!

What good is life without living? *Taste it, live it—* even at the risk of occasional failure and adversity! If you are going to stand at the plate, then take a swing at the ball! "Suppose I miss?" you say. Well, I say, "Suppose you miss out, and you haven't even taken a swing?" Have you any passion to triumph? Your desire to protect yourself from further disappointment has placed you in a comatose state. Wake up and play! You are not dead! There may be many things about you that are dead, but you are not dead!

I feel like God is speaking to someone who has quit. No one knows you have quit, but inside, you have thrown in the towel and said, "I give." You wanted to make a difference, but since you ran into some obstacle, some cross, you decided to adjust your expectations to your limitations and just keep smiling!

You are wrong! I am blowing a trumpet loudly into your *rigor mortis*-ridden ear! *God has too much for you to do!* Arise, breathe deeply of this moment. There will never be another moment in your life like this one! I can't spare you tears, fears, or traumas; each passion has its "cross of validation." In fact, it is the cross that validates the enormity of the passion. *It is what you endure that expresses how deeply you desire.*

*And unto the angel of the church in Sardis
write; These things saith He that hath the seven
Spirits of God, and the seven stars; I know thy
works, that thou hast a name that thou livest,
and art dead. Be watchful, and strengthen the
things which remain, that are ready to die: for I
have not found thy works perfect before God.*
Revelation 3:1-2

## THE PASSION OF JESUS CHRIST

Jesus suffered the loss of His disciples, His earthly ministry, His friends, and even His clothes. They cast lots at His bleeding feet for His seamless robe (see Jn. 19:23-24), but they could not strip away His passion. Even while He was dying He continued to minister His message. He went through hell to reach the joy set before Him, but when He had finished (after His passion), He got up with the keys to death and hell! His trophies were the stinger snatched from death itself and victory yanked from the grave. His prize was a Church purchased by the blood He shed. But what is ultimately important is that He accomplished it with His passion.

*For God so loved the world, that He gave His
only begotten Son, that whosoever believeth in
Him should not perish, but have everlasting
life.* John 3:16

He "so loved" us. That's what He did on the cross; He "so loved" us. This passionate lover, whose Kingdom was not of this world, came to our world and, with unfeigned love, reached into the jaws of damnation and caught my falling soul. His love is exemplified in His coming, but it is consummated in His dying. In His living He betrothed us, but in His dying He procured us.

Jesus Christ, the greatest lover the world has ever known, gives Himself openly and unashamedly. He has found in the cross a mode of expression that becomes a picture of the magnitude of His love. His suffering was a by-product of His passion. His intense love for His ungodly creations led Him to three nails and one tree.

## THE ENEMY'S AGENDA

Where there is no passion, there simply is no power. I fear greatly that the enemy will attempt to either steal the passion or smother it beneath the fear of failure and rejection. If we exist without passion, we slump into a state of stagnation that hinders us from achieving the purpose of God in our lives.

It is the burning effect of a vision that causes us to escape destruction. I repeat, I believe with all my heart that a man never dies with a twinkle in his eye. A gleam of expectation found in the faces of visionaries creates a tenacity that is not easily vanquished. If satan could steal nothing from you but your passion, he would have stolen much of your potency and power in one fell swoop!

The thing you must be aware of, my friend, is that the enemy is trying to steal something from you *that is not visible*. Any time the invisible is stolen, its absence is not readily detected. On what day does passion leave a marriage? On which morning did the worker lose interest in his job? At what point does the customer decide, "I am not going to buy the product"?

Depletion comes when enthusiasm leaks out of a person like air seeping silently out of a tire. Stealthily, the thief siphons life from you like a minute cut saps the strength of the tire. Suddenly, what was meant to roll and bear much weight can now only wobble. There has been such a loss of pressure that what was once inflated has now become deflated.

> *Above all else, guard your heart, for it is the wellspring of life.* Proverbs 4:23 (NIV)

The only solution lies in the absolute, committed guarding of the heart. Your greatest treasure isn't your certificate of deposit. It isn't your retirement, or your stocks and bonds. Your greatest treasure is in the strength of the passion that is locked in the recesses of your heart. Out of the heart flow the issues of life.

You must keep a firm sobriety about you, warming your heart with it like it was a warm coat on a wintry night. Keep a sobriety that refuses to become drunken with fear, discontentment, or insecurity. Wrap your godly attitude closely around your heart, for it is the wellspring or the resource from which comes the strength to keep on living and giving!

## Going Through the Labor

I must be careful to say that you can't spend the rest of your life trying to protect yourself from the struggles of life. They are unavoidable. All men face struggles and the seasons of life, irregardless of their economical, spiritual, or sociological persuasion! If you become intimidated by that fact, it will cause you to live your life in an emotional incubator, insulated but isolated. Having declared that, we must no longer focus on what can be protected. It is not *what we go through* that must be closely monitored. It isn't the pain that we are adamantly resisting—it is *the loss of passion*! We can no more stop pain than we can stop labor pains from coming upon a woman who is in travail!

Look at the birthing table of the expectant mother. It is designed to hold her in the birth position in spite of the pain. Can you maintain your position—even when it means that you will be exposed to a harsh level of pain? That is what good ministry does in our lives. It holds us in place, even when we would have stepped out of the will of God to save ourselves from the stress of the process. Jesus was tied to the birthing table in the garden of Gethsemane. The Church was in Him "from the foundation of the world," and it was to be brought out of His bleeding side on the cross. He was laid in the stirrups in the garden. As the pains became greater, He prayed to change position. He didn't want to be in the vulnerable position of delivery!

> *Saying, Father, if Thou be willing, remove this*
> *cup from Me: nevertheless not My will, but*
> *Thine, be done.* Luke 22:42

We are tied to our destiny like a little trembling lamb is tied to the altar for sacrifice. Like a woman lifted to the birthing bed, trembling in pain, forehead drenched with perspiration—we who are on the verge of miracles are always kept in a perpetual state of vulnerability! If it were not for our passion for an expected end, we would have just fainted away entirely, declaring that the process is too great and the reward too insignificant.

## PASSIONATE PRAYERS OF THE INFIRM

There has to be a certain intensity of desire to empower a person to persevere. Even when we pray, God isn't moved by our vocabulary. He has answered the broken, fragmented prayers of the illiterate mind, whose limited intellect could not abort the childlike faith that produces miracles. He is, as the Scriptures declare, "touched with the feeling of our infirmities" (Heb. 4:15). The passionate God is, in fact, touched by the passions of the prayers of the infirm.

> *For we have not an high priest which cannot be touched with the feeling of our infirmities; but was in all points tempted like as we are, yet without sin.* Hebrews 4:15

The term rendered as "infirmities" is, first of all, mentioned in its plural form to indicate that there is generally more than one. How tragic that most of us will not even admit to the presence of one infirmity, much less the multiplicity of our infirmities. When God is "touched" by them, that means He is *sympathetic* to the feeling of our infirmities.

*Strong's Exhaustive Concordance of the Bible* tells us that the Greek word *astheneia* means "feebleness (of mind or body); by implication, malady; morally, frailty." This is the word that the Authorized Version translates as "infirmities." Somewhere in the most gifted heart, mind, or body, exists some *malady* or *frailty*—whether moral, mental, or physical—that incapacitates us to the degree that we need God's mercies newly bestowed upon us every morning.

## We Are of Like Passions

By God's design, left splayed before us on the pages of the Scriptures, are the intricate details of the life of David, whose passions were both an asset and a liability. We openly filter through his secret thoughts as casually as if we were reading the evening *Times*. His inner struggles and childhood dysfunctions are openly aired on the pages of the text like the center foldout in a tabloid.

God didn't display David's failures in a divine attempt to expose the secret prayers of His struggling king. Rather, His purpose is to give us a point of reference that exhibits the manifold grace of God. How marvelous is the message that instructs us that if God could use a David, He also can use us, as we are all men of *like passions*.

I do not dispute the passions. In fact, without them I can never migrate from the obscure hills and shepherd fields of yesteryear to the victorious acquisition of the palace to which I have been called. Yet I want to issue a point of warning in the midst of this dissertation *to the* one *who dares to lay bare his innermost passions and desires* before God—He who has examined the inner workings of every heart. In reality, in Acts 14:15 the phrase "like passions" comes from the Greek word *homiopathas* which literally translated means "to be similarly affected."

Did you know that God used men who were similarly affected (as you are) by certain stimuli and struggles? What a joy to know that treasure can be surrounded by trash and still not lose its value! Is a diamond less valuable if it is found in a clogged drain? Of course not!

> *And saying, Sirs, why do ye these things? We also are men of like passions with you, and preach unto you that ye should turn from these vanities unto the living God, which made heaven, and earth, and the sea, and all things that are therein.* Acts 14:15

## A WARNING TO THE PASSIONATE

The same passion that makes us very good could potentially make us very bad. Undirected passion becomes a spawning bed for perversity and dankness. It is *what we do with what we feel* that controls the direction of our lives. The same sail that causes a ship to run before an eastward wind through fog and rain can also push it headlong in another direction.

Hear me, O passionate dreamer, whose passion is to walk after God: *The same drive that has become a sword wielded against the enemy, can become a billboard of disgrace if not carefully attended!*

The same John who preached in the desert with power and conviction about the coming of the King and His Kingdom, one day lay trembling on the cold, damp floor of a jail cell, haunted by one question. *Was the Christ he baptized and called "the Lamb of God" really authentic?* Under growing pressure, he finally sent a messenger to ask the infamous question, "Art Thou He that should come, or do we look for another?" (Mt. 11:3)

What a wailing in prayer this truth should elicit from the hearts of men and women! Their God-given passions have delivered them from the mediocrity of constant procrastination and blessed them to achieve. Now they must watch carefully, lest the same serum that made them who they are now perpetuate a downfall! Our defense is naked, honest, fervent prayer. It is the mediatory power of God that so often catches our falling souls and sets us back in the nest with the tenderness of a mother sparrow.

## HE RESTORETH MY SOUL

Passions are to be submitted to the Father, just as our Lord submitted His all on the cross. That is the place where He wielded all of His passion and all of His force— His passion was aimed at the joy set before Him, the target of being a submitted Son. God tested the power of committed passion at Calvary. If it had not been effective, Christ would have had to buy Joseph's tomb instead of borrow it. This is frightening if you read this with the mummylike mentality that preempts most people from accomplishing anything. They *neutralize their passion* with an apathy and unconcern that renders them flaccid and ineffective.

Have you faced some tragedies that almost left you in a state of shock? I can really relate to that feeling. I remember going through a time of complete emptiness in my ministry. My symptoms included a nonchalance and a complete aloofness. I seemed to ignore things that I normally would have straightened out. It was almost as if nothing mattered to me anymore. I built a wall of unconcern to hide the deep depression that had engulfed my life. If you don't usually attend to things with an organized plan, then you won't be able to relate to what I am saying. Normally I am a stickler for details. However, during my time of depression, I became indifferent about whether or not things were done—I simply was "disconnected." It seemed safe to be disconnected because *as long as I didn't care, it didn't hurt*. I had lost the passion to continue. I was completely disenchanted. Have you ever experienced the loss of passion and felt no intensity to be productive?

> *Unto the woman He said, I will greatly multiply thy sorrow and thy conception; in sorrow thou shalt bring forth children; and thy desire shall be to thy husband, and he shall rule over thee.* Genesis 3:16

When God spoke to the first woman about childbirth, He spoke of sorrow and travail. He spoke of the violent, tempestuous pain of labor. He forewarned her about the billowing progression of contractions she would experience at the end of the third trimester of pregnancy. As her pelvic bones are literally moved apart, as if separated by the effects of an earthquake, she is opened as the gates of her femininity prepare for the birth of a child.

The near-deathlike pains come faster and harder as she gets closer to delivery. The soft feminine flesh of the woman whose petals are crushed beneath the weight of an oncoming child is engulfed in a traumatic rush to deliver life. Afterwards, you would expect her to vow never to know another man again!

However, God says that at the end of all this labor and pain, He would recycle the relationship between the woman and the man by the return of desire! He says, "And thy desire shall be to thy husband..." (Gen. 3:16b). God knows that *there is no cure for past pain like present desire.* If the desire is strong enough, the pain of the past will dissipate like bubbles in a glass of water. The wounded and the weary will rise victoriously with new desire, and the cycle continues.

Listen, my friend: Perhaps you have gone through some earthshaking experience that affected and traumatized you. I understand the fear of being hurt again. Once a child has been burned, he will dread fire. But you can't live the rest of your life in fear and dread; *God wants to renew your passion and revive your desire!*

May the passion "to be all that God wants you to be" sweep over your soul like the powerful gusts of a trade wind over a calm sea. As the Bible says, Jesus "shewed Himself alive after His passion by many infallible proofs..." (Acts 1:3). *Do not hide,* my friend. *Show your-self alive with many infallible proofs!* As the passion to continue comes creeping back into your life, resist the temptation to hide behind the fig leaves of past issues. Come out of hiding and show yourself—*naked and not ashamed!*

# *Chapter 5*

## REAPING THE REWARDS OF YOUR OWN THOUGHTS

The streaming fount of holy blood that flows from the gaping wounds of my loving Savior has draped my wretchedness in His holiness. He has covered me like Boaz covered Ruth. He has covered me just like the dripping blood of lambs covered the aged doorposts and lintels of the Hebrew slaves in Egypt on the night of the passover.

His blood also has covered me like a warm blanket on a cold wintry night. I found my past nestled beneath His omnipresent banner of love and concern, taking the chill out of my life and removing the stiffness from my heart. When I had no one to snuggle close to, He became my eternal companion—always seeking out what is best for me and bringing before me great and mighty things.

I confess that I often used to resist loneliness. I filled my life with work and with people who meant me no good at all. At that time, I would rather have filled my life with noise than run the risk of total silence. How foolish of me not to note the difference between being *alone* and being *lonely*.

Have you ever wearied of people? Of course we love the people around us and we enjoy their company, but there comes a time in life that all the fillers we add to avoid emptiness leave us feeling more empty than emptiness could ever be. There is nothing more hollow than empty words and lofty clichés that have no real meaning or compassion in them. They roll listlessly from the mouths of people whose conversations are designed to entertain, but have no capacity to edify.

## A FIRE IN THE WINTER

I recently had the privilege of entertaining my 90-year-old grandmother, whose robust frame and bountiful body has deteriorated to just a mere shadow of its former presence. The arms that were once filled with strength, that once trembled violently while churning butter deep in the state of Mississippi, were now hollow and frail. They felt so brittle in my hands as I supported her faltering frame. Her hair has turned to wisps, reminding me of the angel hair used to decorate our Christmas tree when I was a child. Nevertheless, her spirit seemed strong and graceful.

Grandmother's eyes held within them the burning embers of a fire, embers buried deep beneath the ashes of her experiences. I realized when I looked at her now foreign frame that, beneath her willowy arms and straggling gait, she still possessed more flame in her winter than most people muster in the heat of summer!

She seemed to enjoy my company, and we talked about the old days—about people who were dead and places I only pretended to remember. Her laughter was still there, though it seemed more brittle than I remembered, and it faded more easily. It left behind a faint smile on her face that suggested a thought so private that I yearned to hear what she didn't say much more than what she did say.

I remembered her strong voice with that piercing edge that had once warned us to shut that raggedy screen door she had. I remembered her standing on her old screened-in porch, which was supported by a patchwork of bricks and blocks laced together interchangeably as a foundation to her old farmhouse. She would stand at the old screen door, with its panes shaped into craters, and call us from labor to reward. She would wave at us to come in from the field where we played much more than we worked, to receive her fried chicken and biscuits, baptized in sorghum molasses.

This was the Trojan-like woman who had worked her way through college doing laundry, studying in the wee hours of the night. This was the Mississippi matron who had reached high and hit hard, who captured a teaching degree in the middle of her life and went from canning butter beans to educating children. Now she had come to the setting of the sun.

I could see that sun burning behind her leathery skin and glazed eyes. It seemed that age had somehow smothered her need to talk, and she would lapse into long periods of silence that left me clamoring foolishly through asinine conversations. Whenever I asked her if she was all right, she would respond affirmatively and assure me that she was greatly enjoying my company. Then she would flee into the counsel of her own thoughts and come out at intervals to play with me, with some humorous statement that would remind me of her earlier years.

## A NEW LESSON LEARNED

As I pondered her different behavior and her silent, Indian-like demeanor, I realized that her silence was not boredom. It was, first of all, the mark of someone who has learned how to be *alone*. It reflected the hours she had spent sitting in a rocking chair, entertaining herself with her own thoughts, and reconciling old accounts that brought the past into balance before the books were presented to the Master Himself. My grandmother had prepared her heart for the God who audits our thoughts in the chambers of His own wisdom, and rewards us according to what He finds hidden within us. She had entered into the state where things that seemed so important when you are young and full of days now seem trivial and unimportant. She was at peace, with the kind of peace that comes from a firm faith and deep resolution.

My prayer, as I looked at her, seemed almost envious—not of her failing frame, but of her starched character and calm repose. Her stressless eyes made my anxieties and concerns seem like the foolish ranting of a youthful mind. She calmed me like a sedative taken in the middle of a night. I knew that each time I touched her, I was holding a privilege that would soon expire, and I savored her friendship and love like a dry-mouthed traveler savors a cool glass of water on a hot, blistering day. He knows he will soon swallow it and it will be gone, so he swirls the last sip around and around in his mouth, trying desperately to make the moment last. Though his attempts are futile, his intentions are honorable and they are rewarded with the richness of experience.

So I, too, am rewarded. I am rewarded with a friendly reminder from a loving God who speaks through the glazed eyes of an aged relative, telling me to relax and enjoy life. It was there that I made two commitments in my own mind, as my grandmother smiled and gazed out of a window as if she were looking at Heaven itself. I committed to a renewed faith and trust in the ableness of God. The other commitment I made may seem strange, but I promised to spend more time with myself, to warm myself at the fire of my own thoughts and smile with the contentments of the riches contained therein.

## HEALING OF THE MIND

*Let the words of my mouth, and the meditation*
*of my heart, be acceptable in Thy sight, O*
*Lord, my strength, and my redeemer.*
Psalm 19:14

We must understand that modern medicine can heal many afflictions of the body, and can even treat the tumors that sometimes attach themselves to the brain, but only God Himself can heal the mind. Do you know that many times your *thoughts* need to be healed? Your thoughts are often the product of damaged emotions, traumatic events, and vicious opinions forced upon you by the bodacious personalities of domineering people who continually feel it necessary to express their opinions about you.

One of the great challenges of our walk with God is to resist the temptation to allow what happened in the past determine who we are today. We each must begin to understand and declare: "I am not what happened yesterday. I *endured* what happened. I *survived* what happened, but *I am not what happened* yesterday!"

Many people are plagued all their lives by memories of failed marriages, broken promises, and personal calamities. They have allowed past events to eat at their thoughts like a cancer—a cancer that defies medical technology and continues to devour its victim in an area that the doctor cannot find. These negative impressions, armed with memories and flashback "movies," strengthen themselves by rehearsing past failures and wounds over and over again. It is somehow like bad television reruns—we don't even enjoy watching them, yet we find ourselves transfixed to the screen. Almost tied to the chair, as if some captor was holding us down, we have to remind ourselves about the "remote control" and free ourselves from the bondage of watching things that do not entertain us.

In the same sense, you must remind yourself that you don't have to watch the "movie" in your mind if you are not enjoying what is being played. That's right—hit the remote control. You *do have control* over your thoughts. The Bible teaches us that if we are going to be healed in our own mind, then we must occasionally reprogram ourselves to "think on better thoughts."

> *Finally, brethren, whatsoever things are true,*
> *whatsoever things are honest, whatsoever*
> *things are just, whatsoever things are pure,*
> *whatsoever things are lovely, whatsoever*
> *things are of good report; if there be any*
> *virtue, and if there be any praise, think on*
> *these things.* Philippians 4:8

You must choose what you are going to meditate upon. Choose carefully, though, for *you will ultimately become whatever it is you meditate upon.* The enemy knows this, so when he wants to destroy your morality, he doesn't start with an act; he starts with a thought. A thought is a seed that, if not aborted, will produce off-spring somewhere in your life.

## SEEDS OF EVIL THOUGHTS

Satan plants seeds in the form of thoughts. These evil seeds aren't yours just because they come to mind; they become yours when you allow those thoughts to move in and rearrange furniture! An evil thought will rearrange your goals, your dreams, and your ambitions (that is a *very powerful* house guest). A thought left to ramble in your mind will attach itself to an incident in your past. It will begin to feed on that incident and grow like a tick that attaches itself to your body while you walk through a forest. That thing isn't a part of your body, but it begins by attaching itself to the body and then drains strength from it.

These evil thoughts impede progress and destroy morals. They are as dangerous as the act of sin itself. Thoughts are previews of coming attractions. That is why Jesus gave us some strong teachings about lust. He knew that if an evil thought is not aborted, if it is savored long enough, it will be acted upon!

> *You have heard that it was said, "Do not com-*
> *mit adultery." But I tell you that anyone who*
> *looks at a woman lustfully has already commit-*
> *ted adultery with her in his heart.*
> Matthew 5:27-28 (NIV)

You must quickly cast down an evil thought. "Push the remote control" before it drains away your commitment to excellence and leaves you crying in the valley of regret. The real temptation to entertain thoughts is in the privacy of the mind. Who will know what you really think? You can smile at people and never disclose your innermost thoughts.

I always laugh when I see people act as though they have conquered the battle with the mind. I've asked people in my services, "Which of you would be comfortable with having everything that comes to mind played on a television screen for all of your Christian friends to watch? Or which of you would like to have all our thoughts through the week played over the loudspeaker at church next Sunday?" I'm sure I don't have to tell you, they all put their hands down. Our mind is a private battleground that can easily become a secret place for contamination, lust, fear, low self-esteem, and God only knows what else!

When we clean our homes we tend to focus our efforts first on what people will see rather than on what they will not see. Only the most ardent of housekeepers spends as much time scrubbing the basement steps as she does the foyer or the living room. We emphasize what will be inspected.

Can you imagine how much clutter we allow to fester in our minds, simply because no one sits in our heads sipping tea and examining the thoughts and imaginations of our hearts? If no one knows what we think, why shouldn't we allow our minds to collect scum and clutter without any regard to cleaning and renewing the mind? There are several reasons not to do that, but I will give only three.

## GOD KNOWS

First, a certain *Someone does know what we think.* God sits in the living quarters of the minds of men and beholds their thoughts. He knows our thoughts afar off (see Ps. 139:2). If we are serious about entertaining His presence, we cannot lie to Him—He sees us from the inside out. We must be honest and admit to Him:

*This is what I am being tempted with...I cannot hide from You. I am naked before You. All my thoughts are played on the screen before You. I want to clean up this*

59

mess so You can replace it with a greater revelation and a stronger direction for my life. I praise You for loving me, in spite of all You know about me. Forgive me for condemning and judging anybody else. I know that if it were not for Your mercy, I would be guilty of the very things for which I have disdained others. Help me not to be hypocritical.

This kind of prayer and confession enhances your relationship with God as you begin to realize that you *were* saved by grace; you *are* saved by grace; and you *will be* saved by grace! Knowing this, how can you not be grateful? You know that He loves you so much that He stays in the house you haven't fully cleaned. He hates the acts; He despises the thoughts; but He loves the thinker.

> *Neither is there any creature that is not manifest in His sight: but all things are naked and opened unto the eyes of Him with whom we have to do. Seeing then that we have a great high priest, that is passed into the heavens, Jesus the Son of God, let us hold fast our profession. For we have not an high priest which cannot be touched with the feeling of our infirmities; but was in all points tempted like as we are, yet without sin.* Hebrews 4:13-15

Immediately after the writer of the Book of Hebrews tells us that God knows all our business and that all our thoughts parade around naked before His scrutinizing eyes, he mentions the high priest that we have in Christ. He knows we are going to need a high priest for all the garbage and information that the Holy Spirit is privy to, yet others would never know. What greater compassion can be displayed than when the writer goes on to say that God, through Christ, can be *touched by how I feel*. No wonder Jeremiah said His mercies are "new every morning"! (See Lamentations 3:22-23.)

## WE ARE WHAT WE THINK

Second, we need to continually purge our thoughts because *we become what we think*. It is not just the lust that we must clean out, but also low self-esteem, pride, arrogance, hidden jealousy, and much, much more. The mind is the "placenta" of the spirit man. It holds and nurtures the seeds it has been impregnated with until their time of delivery. If you don't want the child that that seed of thought produces, your only recourse is to abort before it is carried to full term.

If you don't want depression, why do you continue to regurgitate those same sickening thoughts that lead you down the tunnel of emotional depravity? You don't need a famous minister to lay hands on you to win the battle over your mind! The truth is, generally speaking, those fantastic demonstrations of public power seldom accomplish deliverance from mental images. What you need is the inner discipline required of all disciples to resist evil thoughts before they become evidenced in your life.

Most people who are unsuccessful in their lives do not lack talent. Some of the most talented people I have ever known weren't successful, even in the area of their talent. Why? There always seemed to be some little thought they entertained that affected their tenacity or their commitment to excellence. Some dwarfed self-image, or worse still, some over-inflated ego preempted them from reaching their aspirations and sent them plummeting to the ground of failure and the rocks of frustration. If you can see traces of this in your own life (and most of us can), abort the seeds that are causing you to miss the mark and press on! Don't you realize that anything you stop feeding is sure to die?!

> *(For the weapons of our warfare are not carnal,*
> *but mighty through God to the pulling down*
> *of strong holds;) casting down imaginations,*
> *and every high thing that exalteth itself against*
> *the knowledge of God, and bringing into cap-*
> *tivity every thought to the obedience of Christ.*
> 2 Corinthians 10:4-5

The mind is continually being reconstructed by the Holy Spirit. He wants to perpetuate a new mentality within you that enables you to soar above your past. He impregnates us with hope and fills us with destiny. The Scriptures challenge us with the exhortation, "Let this mind be in you, which was also in Christ Jesus: who, being in the form of God, thought it not robbery to be equal with God: but made Himself of no reputation..." (Phil. 2:5-7).

Simply stated, Christ has a balanced mind. He doesn't suffer from low self-esteem. He "thought it not robbery" to be equal with God. For Him, being equal with God was and is a reality. That might be a little extreme for you and me, but the point is that He was comfortable with

His exaltation. He didn't allow the controversial opinions of other men to determine who He "thought" He was. His inner perception was fixed.

The miracle of His strength is that, unlike most people who are that strong about their inner worth, Christ Jesus did not wrestle with arrogance. He knew who He was, yet He "made Himself of no reputation" (Phil. 2:7a). When you have healthy thoughts about your own identity, it frees you from the need to impress other people. Their opinion ceases to be the shrine where you worship!

Most of us come to the Lord damaged. We're dead spiritually, damaged emotionally, and decaying physically. When He saved you, He quickened, or made alive, your dead spirit. He also promised you a new body. Then He began the massive renovation necessary to repair your damaged thoughts about life, about others, and about yourself—here come all types of nails, saws, levels, bricks, and blocks.

While we dress and smell nice outwardly, people do not hear the constant hammering and sawing going on inwardly, as the Lord works within us, trying desperately to meet a deadline and present us as a newly constructed masterpiece fit for the Master's use.

*For we are His workmanship, created in Christ Jesus unto good works, which God hath before ordained that we should walk in them.*
Ephesians 2:10

Beneath our pasted smiles and pleasant greetings, we alone hear the rumblings of the midnight shift. God is constantly excommunicating lethal thoughts that hinder us from grasping the many-faceted callings and giftings buried beneath the rubble of our minds. No matter who we meet, once we get to know them, we begin to realize that they have their own challenges. Have you ever met someone and thought he had it all together? Once you become closely involved with that person, you will begin to notice a twisted board here, a loose nail there, or even a squeaky frame!

Yes, we all need the Lord to help us with ourselves. We came to Him as condemned buildings, and He reopened the places that satan thought would never be inhabited. The Holy Spirit moved in, but He brought His hammers and His saw with Him. He will challenge the thoughts of men.

## To Become More Like Him

Third, we need to renew our minds daily in God's presence, for I believe that *as we hear the thoughts of God, His thinking becomes increasingly contagious.* It is so important that we have a relationship with Him. His Word becomes a lifeline thrown to a man who would otherwise drown in the swirling whirlpool of his own thoughts. Peter was so addicted to hearing Jesus speak that when other men walked away, Peter said, "Lord, to whom shall we go? Thou hast the words of eternal life" (Jn. 6:68).

Peter recognized his need to keep hearing the Word of God. Many years before Peter, Job said that he esteemed God's Word more than his necessary food (see Job 23:12). As for me, God is my counselor. He talks with me about my deepest, darkest issues; He comforts the raging tide of my fears and inhibitions. What would we be if He would wax silent and cease to guide us through this perilous maze of mental mania? It is His soft words that turn away the wrath of our nagging memories. If He speaks to me, His words become symphonies of enlightenment falling like soft rain on a tin roof. They give rest and peace.

*For My thoughts are not your thoughts, neither are your ways My ways, saith the Lord. For as the heavens are higher than the earth, so are My ways higher than your ways, and My thoughts than your thoughts. For as the rain cometh down, and the snow from heaven, and returneth not thither, but watereth the earth, and maketh it bring forth and bud, that it may give seed to the sower, and bread to the eater: so shall My word be that goeth forth out of My mouth: it shall not return unto Me void, but it shall accomplish that which I please, and it shall prosper in the thing whereto I sent it. For ye shall go out with joy, and be led forth with peace: the mountains and the hills shall break forth before you into singing, and all the trees of the field shall clap their hands. Instead of the thorn shall come up the fir tree, and instead of the brier shall come up the myrtle tree: and*

*it shall be to the Lord for a name, for an ever-
lasting sign that shall not be cut off.*
Isaiah 55:8-13

God's Word will accomplish what it is sent out to do.
God says, "I won't stop in the middle of the job. I will not
give up on you. I will keep hammering until you are balanced in your thinking and whole in your judgments."
The greatest part is, no one would ever believe that you
were initially in such a deplorable state! He covers you
with His precious blood even while His Word works on
you. The benefit is that you are simultaneously *privileged
with privacy* and *challenged to change.*

In a world where people seem void of commitment
and so easily become distracted, it is comforting to know
that God won't give up on you. He will persevere and
labor with you until His will is accomplished in your life.
If anybody ought to praise the Lord, it ought to be those
who have a deep appreciation for His unfailing love. It is
to them He has spoken His word and changed their
thoughts and directions. He has healed the bitter waters
of a turbulent mind!

Human thoughts are healed by the Word of God. By
the "foolishness of preaching" (see 1 Cor. 1:21), God filters
into the dark places of our diseased or oppressed minds
and reconstructs thought patterns by sharing His own
mind with us. We must, at all cost, maintain an appetite
for preaching. Why? "So then faith [a change of mind]
cometh by hearing, and hearing by the word of God"
(Rom. 10:17). It boggles the mind of secular scholars to see
the power of God's Word transforming dysfunctional

members of our society into productive and affluent parts of our community. They are amazed—and that is without knowing our whole stories.

Most of the time God delivers us (or is in the process of delivering us) while we maintain a veil of secrecy to protect our reputations and public perceptions. These secular scholars would be appalled if they knew how many of us were in serious trouble when we came to our wit's end and submitted to the redemptive work of the Lord. It was He who delivered us out from under the stress and the strain of our crises. His power forces open the fowler's snare that entrapped the mind. His Word gives us the grace to seize the opportunity to escape and go on with our lives!

> *He sent forth His word and healed them; He rescued them from the grave. Let them give thanks to the Lord for His unfailing love and His wonderful deeds for men.*
> Psalm 107:20-21 (NIV)

## THOUGHTS RESULT IN ACTIONS

As we journey deeper into the dregs of this subject, let us consider the power of thought itself. There is a strong tie between thought and action. Some time ago, when we discovered the power of our words, we began to teach Christians to speak positively. That is good. The only problem is, we were *thinking* one thing while the mouth was *confessing* something else. The results were not rewarding.

The Scriptures tell us that "with the heart man believeth unto righteousness; and with the mouth confession is made unto salvation" (Rom. 10:10). There is a strong tie between what is believed and what is confessed. Your thoughts have to align with your confession—otherwise your house is divided against itself! Even God works out of the reservoir of His own thoughts. He does not consider what others think about you. Some of those people don't even believe in God. Nevertheless, He doesn't work out of their thoughts; He works out of His own! Quit trying to change the minds of other people—change your own. Your works will come out of the healing of your thoughts!

> *How great are Your works, O Lord, how pro-*
> *found Your thoughts!* Psalm 92:5 (NIV)

Yes, our God is reaping the rewards of His own thoughts—and so are you. Whether that is good or bad depends on what you are thinking. Whether you are thinking of a secret lust that will eventually become fornication, or thinking of violent aggression that will become an act of physical domination over another, you are reaping the rewards of your own thoughts. No wonder the Bible warns us, "Where there is no vision, the people perish" (Prov. 29:18a)!

You need to allow new meditations to dwell in your heart by faith, for your life will ultimately take on the direction of your thinking. Many weaknesses, such as procrastination and laziness, are just draperies that cover up poor self-esteem and a lack of motivation. They are often symptoms of the subconscious avoiding the risk of failure. Remember that "nothing shall be impossible unto you" if you will only believe! (See Matthew 17:20.)

God creates by speaking, but He speaks out of His own thoughts. Since God's Word says "out of the abundance of the heart the mouth speaketh" (Mt. 12:34b), then we go beyond the mouth to bring correction to the words we speak. We have to begin with the thoughts we think.

I pray that somehow the Spirit will reveal the areas where you need Him to heal your thinking so you can possess what God wants you to have. Then you will be able to fully enjoy what He has given you. Many people have the blessing and still don't enjoy it because they conquered every foe *except the enemy within*!

> *The Lord of hosts hath sworn, saying, Surely as I have thought, so shall it come to pass; and as I have purposed, so shall it stand.* Isaiah 14:24

## YOUR PERCEPTION COUNTS

When at King David's command Ziba returned from Lodebar with Mephibosheth, the crippled son of Jonathan, to David's palace, Mephibosheth couldn't sit at the table without falling to the floor. He struggled with his position because of his condition. His problem wasn't merely his twisted feet or his crippled body. It was his dysfunctional mentality. Even after he had been raised from the deplorable condition he was in, he was still so oppressed in his mind that he described himself as a "dead dog" (see 2 Sam. 9:8). He was a king's kid, but he saw himself as a dead dog!

Perception is everything. Mephibosheth thought of himself as a dead dog, so he lay on the floor like one. I feel a word going out from the Lord to you: *You have been on the floor long enough!* It is time for a resurrection, and it is going to start in your *mind*. Has God blessed you with something you are afraid of losing? Could it be that you think you are going to lose it because you don't feel worthy? I realize that living in the palace can be a real shock to someone who is accustomed to being rejected and ostracized. Without realizing it, you will accept being treated as though you were a dog. Mephibosheth had been through so much that he began to think himself a dead dog.

Understand this one fact: *Just because you've been treated like a dog doesn't make you one!* Get up off the floor and take a seat at the Master's table—you are worthy. You have a right to be in the place and position you are in, not because of your goodness, but by virtue of His invitation. I pray that God will heal your thoughts until you are able to enjoy and rest in what God is doing in your life right now!

## KEEP THOSE SEEDS!

Your confession is great. You've fought and defended yourself against attackers, and you have seen some increase; but when you allow God to heal your thoughts, you will explode into another dimension. Sometimes we have been strong because we had great struggles. We fought valiantly in the face of the enemies of life. However, when sunset falls on the battlefield, and after the troops have gone home, we hang up our gear and wish we were as valiant inwardly as we displayed outwardly! Perceive and believe what God is doing in you. If you can get that in your head, you can reap it in your life!

The harvest field that God wants to plant is in your head. Amidst all your troubles, hold onto your field of dreams. If you can water your own field when men are trying to command a drought in your life, God will mightily sustain you. Now I know why my grandmother smiled quietly and looked distantly. She had learned the art of being her own company. She had learned how to irrigate her own mind and entertain her own hours. She was simply self-reliant, not independent (we all need other people). She had learned how to rely on her own thoughts, how to motivate her own smiles, and how to find a place of confidence and serenity within herself as she privately communed with God. There is still much to be accomplished in the person who has maintained thoughts of greatness in the midst of degrading dilemmas. These are the smiles that paint the faces of people who know something greater and deeper, who see beyond their circumstances. They look out of the window, but they see far down the road.

If in your thoughts you see something beyond where you are, if you see a dream, a goal, or an aspiration that others would think impossible, you may have to *hold it.* Sometimes you may have to *hide it,* and most of the time you will have to *water it* as a farmer waters his crops to sustain the life in them. But always remember they are your fields. You must eat from the garden of your own thoughts, so don't grow anything you don't want to eat. As you ponder and daydream, receive grace for the hard places and healing for the damaged soil. Just know that whenever your children, your friends, or anyone else comes to the table of your wisdom, you can only feed them *what you have grown in your own fields*. Your wisdom is so flavorful and its texture so rich that it can't be "store bought"; it must be *homegrown*.

A whispering prayer lies on my lips: *I pray that this word God has given me be so powerful and personal, so intimate and applicable, that it leaves behind it a barren mind made pregnant. This seed of greatness will explode in your life and harvest in your children, feeding the generations to come and changing the winds of destiny.*

As I move on to other issues and as we face our inner selves, we strip away our facades and see ourselves as we really are. I am not fearful of our nakedness nor discouraged by our flaws. I see the dark rich potentials of Son-drenched minds, and I recognize the fragrance in the atmosphere right now. Breathe deeply. Don't you remember that aroma? You can feel it through the pores of your skin.

In my heart I smell the indescribable smell of an approaching rain. Moisture is in the air and the clouds have gathered. Our fields have been chosen for the next rain and the wind has already started to blow. Run swiftly into the field with your precious seeds and plant them in the soft ground of your fertile mind. Whatever you plant in the evening will be reaped in the morning. My friend, I am so excited for you. I just heard a clap of thunder…in just another moment, there'll be rain!

$\mathscr{C}$hapter 6

## THE COLD KISS OF A
## CALLOUSED HEART

Friendship is the last remaining sign of our fleeting childhood dreams. It is the final symptom of our youth that lingers around the shadows of our adult mind. It reminds us of the sweet taste of a *chosen love*. Different from family love, which is not chosen but accepted, this love develops like moss on the slippery edges of a creek. It emerges without warning. There is no date to remember. It just gradually grows until one day an acquaintance has graduated into a friend. Love is the graduation diploma, whether discussed or hinted.

It is real and powerful, sweet and bitter. It is fanciful, idealistic, and iridescent enough to shine in the chilly night of an aloof world that has somehow lost the ability to interpret or appreciate the value of a friend. Only occasionally in the course of a lifetime do we meet the kind of friend that is more than an acquaintance. This kind of kindred spirit feels as warm and fitting as an old house shoe, with its personalized contours impressed upon soft fabric for the benefit of weary feet.

## THE SEARCH FOR TRUE FRIENDSHIP

The tragedy is that we all yearn for, but seldom acquire, true trust and covenant. The truth is that *real relationship is hard work*. Let no man deceive you; contouring the heart to beat with another requires extensive whittling to trim away the self-centeredness with which many of us have enveloped ourselves. It is like riding the bus. If you are going to have company riding with you, you must be willing to scoot over and rearrange to accommodate another person and the many parcels that he brings. Your actions in doing this express the importance of the other person.

Every relationship undergoes adjustments. The reason one relationship becomes more valuable than others is found in its ability to survive circumstances and endure realignments. We never know the magnitude of a relationship's strength until it is tested by some threatening force. There must be a strong adhesive that can withstand the pressure and not be weakened by outside forces.

## FRIENDS DESPITE IMPERFECTIONS

Isn't that part of what we want from relationships? To know that *you won't leave*, regardless of what is encountered—even if you discover my worst imperfection and I disclose my deepest scars! Isn't the real question, "Can I be transparent with you, and be assured that my nudity has not altered your commitment to be my friend?" I know that someone reading this chapter has given up on friendship, with its many expenses and desertions. If you will not believe me, then believe the Word of God. It is possible to attain real abiding friendship.

> A man of many companions may come to ruin,
> but there is a friend who sticks closer than a
> brother. Proverbs 18:24 (NIV)

Incidentally, notice that this proverb clearly warns against *many* companions. It is dangerous to be polygamous—even with friendship. Having too many companions creates jealousy, absorbs time, and cheapens commitment. How many friends can you handle? The object is quality and not quantity. As we share with one another, we must be prepared to love each other's imperfections, even when those imperfections challenge our commitment. We must decide, at some point, whether or not we can love like God. God sees every imperfection we have (He cannot be deceived), yet He maintains His commitment to love the unlovely. Isn't that why we love Him so much? We are completely vulnerable to Him. He knows us, yet He understands and loves us!

Even natural blood ties don't always wear as well as heart ties. The Bible says there is a kind of friend that "sticketh closer than a brother" (Prov. 18:24b). What a tremendous statement. This is why we must not allow our friendships to be easily uprooted—not only in our individual lives, but also collectively as the Body of Christ. Too often we have thrown away good people who did a bad thing. The tragedy is in the fact that we usually forget all the good a friend has done and dwell only on the one bad thing he did to damage us. Have you ever done something like that? The deeper question is this: Are you throwing away the whole car over a bad battery? Is there any possibility of repair? No way, huh? Then how does God ever love you? If He ever forgave you of your debts *as you forgave your debtors*, could you stand?

The obvious friend is the one who stands by you, honoring and affirming you. The obvious friend affirms your marriage and family. You cannot be a friend and not uphold the institution of marriage and family. A true friend should desire to see me prosper in my marriage, in my finances, and in my health and spirituality. If these virtues are present in the relationship, then we can easily climb over the hurdles of personal imperfection and, generally, are mature enough to support what supports us. We, in turn, transmit through fleeting smiles, handshakes, hugs and warm exchanges of mutual affection, our celebration of friendship and appreciation.

## ACCEPTANCE WITHOUT MEASURE

What we all need is *the unique gift of acceptance.* Most of us fear the bitter taste of rejection, but perhaps worse than rejection is the naked pain that attacks an exposed heart when a relationship is challenged by some struggle.

Suppose I share my heart, my innermost thoughts, with someone who betrays me, and I am wounded again? The distress of betrayal can become a wall that insulates us, but it also isolates us from those around us. Yes, I must admit that there are good reasons for being protective and careful. I also admit that love is always a risk. Yet I still suggest that *the risk is worth the reward!* What a privilege to have savored the contemplations of idle moments with the tender eyes of someone whose glistening expression invites you like the glowing embers of a crackling fire.

Communication becomes needless between people who need no audible speech. Their speech is the quick glance and the soft pat on a shoulder. Their communication is a concerned glance when all is not well with you. If you have ever sunken down into the rich lather of a real covenant relationship, then you are wealthy.

This relationship is the wealth that causes street people to smile in the rain and laugh in the snow. They have no coats to warm them; their only flame is the friendship of someone who relates to the plight of daily living. In this regard, many wealthy people are impoverished. They have things, but they lack camaraderie. The greatest blessings are often void of expense, yet they provide memories that enrich the credibility of life's dreary existence.

> *You say, "I am rich; I have acquired wealth and do not need a thing." But you do not realize that you are wretched, pitiful, poor, blind and naked.* Revelation 3:17 (NIV)

Children understand the rich art of relationship. They are often angry, but their anger quickly dissipates in the glaring sunshine of a fresh opportunity to laugh and jest a day away. The hearts of most adults, however, have been blackened by unforgiveness. They will hold a club of remembered infractions against one another for long periods of time, perhaps for a lifetime. There is a vacancy in the hearts of most men that causes them to be narrow and superficial. This vacancy is the vast gap between casual relationships and intimate attachments. It is the gift of friendship that should fill the gap between these wide designated points of human relationship.

## A COMMON BOND

Since there is no blood to form the basis of relativity between friends, the bond must exist through some other mode of reality. A commonality is needed to anchor the relationship of two individuals against the chilly winds of passing observers, whose suspicious minds activate and attempt to terminate any of your relationships. They are not accustomed to relationships outside of the junglelike, carnivorous stalkings of one another as prey. However, this bond may exist in an area that outsiders would never understand, but thank God their confusion doesn't dilute the intensity of admiration that exists between true friends.

Many people are surrounded by crowds of business people, coworkers, and even family members—yet they are alone. Disenchanted with life, they become professional actors on the stage of life. They do not allow anyone to get close, fearing to risk the pain and bleeding of a disappointed heart. Whether they be battered wives or distraught husbands, some among us have given up—not daring to be transparent with anyone for any reason. These have decided to present a fictitious, fragmented appearance among us that never solidifies or really alters us in any way!

I must admit there is no shield for broken hearts that will protect us from the flaws of those whom we dare to befriend. At best, there will be times of trembling need and emotional debates, yet *we need to make the investment* and even face the risk of depletion rather than live in a glass bubble all our lives!

## IT IS PART OF YOUR DESTINY

I know that betrayal can be painful. It is hard to receive disloyalty from hands and hearts you trusted. The fear of a "Judas" has caused many preachers, leaders, as well as the general masses to avoid the attack. Now if you understand anything about God, then you know that *God can give direction out of rejection.* It was Judas' ministry that brought Christ to the cross! Although this betrayal was painful, it was an essential part of His destiny.

It is important to understand destiny as it relates to relationships. God is too wise to have His plans aborted by the petty acts of men. We have to rely on God's divine administration as we become involved with people. Their access to our future is limited by the shield of divine purpose that God Himself has placed on our lives!

> *I hate double-minded men, but I love Your*
> *law. You are my refuge and my shield; I have*
> *put my hope in Your word.*
> Psalm 119:113-114 (NIV)

The extent of damage that mortal men can do to the upright is limited by the purposes of God. What a privilege it is to know that and understand it in your heart. It destroys the constant paranoia that restricts many of us from exploring possible friendships and covenant relationships. Let me be very clear, though; the possibility of getting hurt in a relationship is always present. Any time you make an investment, there is the possibility of a loss. But there is a difference between being hurt and being altered or destroyed.

You belong to God, and He watches over you every day. He monitors your affairs, and acts as your protection. Sometimes He opens doors (we always get excited about God opening doors). But the same God who opens doors also closes doors. I am, perhaps, more grateful for the doors He has closed in my life than I am for the ones He has opened. Had I been allowed to enter some of the doors He closed, I would surely have been destroyed! God doesn't intend for every relationship to flourish. There are some human cliques and social groups in which He doesn't want you to be included!

## GOD WORKS FOR YOUR GOOD

*And to the angel of the church in Philadelphia write; These things saith He that is holy, He that is true, He that hath the key of David, He that openeth, and no man shutteth; and shutteth, and no man openeth. Revelation 3:7*

The letter to the Philadelphia church, the church of brotherly love, basically ends with the words, "I am the

One who closes doors." The art to surviving painful moments is living in the "yes" zone. We need to learn to respond to God with a *yes* when the doors are open, and a *yes* when they are closed. Our prayer must be:

*I trust Your decisions, Lord; and I know that if this relationship is good for me, You will allow it to continue. I know that if the door is closed, then it is also for my good. So I say "yes" to You as I go into this relationship. I appreciate brotherly love, and I still say "yes" if You close the door.*

This is the epitome of a trust that is seldom achieved, but is to be greatly sought after. In so doing, you will be able to savor the gift of companionship without the fear of reprisal!

If God allows a relationship to continue, and some negative, painful betrayals come from it, you must realize that He will only allow what ultimately works *for your good.* Sometimes such a betrayal ushers you into the next level of consecration, a level you could never reach on your own. For that we give thanks! What a privilege to live in the assurance that God is in control of you, and of everyone whom He allows to get behind "the shield" of His purposes for your life! He intimately knows every person whom He cherishes enough to call His child. Any good parent tries to ensure that his or her children are surrounded by positive influences. The unique thing about God's parenting is that He sometimes uses a negative to bring about a positive. If no good can come out of a relationship or situation, then God will not allow it. This knowledge sets us free from internal struggle and allows us to be transparent.

> *Every good gift and every perfect gift is from*
> *above, and cometh down from the Father of*
> *lights, with whom is no variableness, neither*
> *shadow of turning.* James 1:17

If you don't understand the sovereignty of God, then all is lost. There must be an inner awareness within your heart, a deep knowledge that God *is in control* and that *He is able to reverse the adverse.* When we believe in His sovereignty, we can overcome every humanly induced trial because we realize that they are divinely permitted and supernaturally orchestrated. He orchestrates them in such a way that the things that could have paralyzed us only motivate us.

God delights in bestowing His abundant grace upon us so we can live with men *without fear.* In Christ, we come to the table of human relationships feeling like we are standing before a great "smorgasbord" or buffet table. There will be some relationships whose "taste" we prefer over others, but the richness of life is in the opportunity to explore the options. What a dull plate we would face if everything on it was duplicated without distinction. God creates different types of people, and all are His handiwork.

Even in the most harmonious of relationships there are injuries and adversity. If you live in a cocoon, you will miss all the different levels of love God has for you. God allows different people to come into your life to accomplish His purposes. Your friends are ultimately the ones who will help you become all that God wants you to be in Him. When you consider it in that light, you have many friends—some of them expressed friends, and some implied friends.

## JUDAS—A FRIEND?

Implied friendship describes your relationship with those who weren't consciously or obviously trying to help you, yet their actions—though painful—were ultimately purposeful. Therefore, we glory in tribulation! We now understand that God used their negativity to accomplish His will for our lives. Now, because our ultimate goal is to please Him, we must widen our definition of friendship *to include the betrayer* if his betrayal ushered us into the next step of God's plan for our lives.

> *And forthwith he came to Jesus, and said, Hail, master; and kissed Him. And Jesus said unto him, **Friend, wherefore art thou come?** Then came they, and laid hands on Jesus, and took Him. And, behold, one of them which were with Jesus stretched out his hand, and drew his sword, and struck a servant of the high priest's, and smote off his ear. Then said Jesus unto him, Put up again thy sword into his place: for all they that take the sword shall perish with the sword. Thinkest thou that I cannot now pray to My Father, and He shall presently give Me more than twelve legions of angels? But how then shall the scriptures be fulfilled, that thus it must be?* Matthew 26:49-54

83

I understand that in its narrow sense, a friend is one who has good intentions. However, because of the sovereignty of God, I have come to realize that there are some who were actually instrumental in my blessing, although they never really embraced or affirmed me as a person! They played a crucial part in my well-being. These kinds of "friends" are the "Judas sector" that exists in the life of every child of God.

Every child of God not only has, but also *desperately needs*, a "Judas" to carry out certain aspects of divine providence in his life! In the passage quoted above, Judas was more of a friend than Peter! Although Peter was certainly more amiable and admirable, Judas was the one God selected to usher in the next step of the process. Peter's love was almost a deterrent to the purpose of God. Sometimes your friends are the ones who can cause you the most pain. They wound you and betray you, but through their betrayal God's will can be executed in your life.

Judas was no mistake. He was handpicked and selected. His role was crucial to the death and resurrection of Christ. No one helped Christ reach His goal like Judas. If God allowed certain types of people to come into our lives, they would hinder us from His divine purpose. "Thank You, Lord, for my mysterious friends whose venomous assault led me to lean on You more explicitly than I would have, had they not tried to destroy me!" This is the prayer of the seasoned heart that has been exercised by the tragedies of life. It has reduced and controlled the fatty feelings and emotions that cause us to always seek those whose actions tickle our ears.

We all want to be surrounded by a friend like John, whose loving head lay firmly on Jesus' breast. We may long for the protective instincts of a friend like Peter, who stood ready to attack every negative force that would come against Jesus. In his misdirected love, Peter even withstood Jesus to His face over His determination to die for mankind. But the truth of the matter is, Jesus could have accomplished His goal without Peter, James, or John; but *without Judas He would never have reached the hope of His calling!*

Leave my Judas alone. I need him in my life. He is my mysterious friend, the one who aids me without even knowing it. When you encounter a Judas in your life, remember that it is his actions that carry out the purpose of God in your life! Look back over your life and understand that it is persecution that strengthens you. It is the struggles and the trauma we face that help us persevere.

Thank God for your friends and family and their support, but remember that it is often your relationship with that mysterious friend of malice and strife, weakness and defective behavior, that becomes the catalyst for greatness in your life! It is much easier to forgive the actions of men when you know the purposes of God! Not only should we refuse to fear their actions—we should release them.

What happens when friendship takes an unusual form? Did you know that God, our ultimate Friend, sometimes manipulates the actions of our enemies to cause them to work as friends in order to accomplish His will in our lives? *God can bless you through the worst of relationships!* That is why we must learn how to accept even the relationships that seem to be painful or negative. The time, effort, and pain we invest in them is not wasted because *God knows how to make adversity feed destiny into your life!*

In short, the bleeding trail of broken hearts and wounded relationships ultimately leads us to the richness of God's purpose in us. Periodically each of us will hear a knock on the door. It is the knock of our old friend Judas, whose cold kiss and calloused heart usher us into the will of God. To be sure, these betrayals call bloody tears to our eyes and nail us to a cold cross. Nevertheless, the sweet kiss of betrayal can never abort the precious promises of God in our life! The challenge is to sit at the table with Judas on one side and John on the other, and to treat one no differently from the other, even though we are distinctly aware of each one's identity and agenda. If you have been betrayed or wounded by someone you brought too close, please forgive them. They really were a blessing. You will only be better when you cease to be bitter!

> *It is good for me that I have been afflicted; that I might learn Thy statutes.* Psalm 119:71

I cannot stop your hurts from coming; neither can I promise that everyone who sits at the table with you is loyal. But I can suggest that the sufferings of success give us direction and build character within us. Finally, as you find the grace to reevaluate your enemies and realize that many of them were friends in disguise, I can only place a warm hand of solace on your sobbing shoulders and wipe the gentle rain of soft tears from your eyes. As God heals what hurt you have, I want to whisper gently in your ears, "Betrayal is only sweetened when it is accompanied by survival. Live on, my friend, live on!"

# *Chapter 7*

## SURVIVE THE CRASH OF RELATIONSHIPS

There is a deep-seated need in all of us to sense purpose—even out of calamity. Out of this thirst for meaning is born the simplistic yet crucial prayer, "*Why?*" Most of us have faced tense moments where this urgent prayer has exploded from our lips. It is a cry for purpose, not solutions. It suggests that if we can only find meaning to the madness, then the strength to endure would quickly rise up in us.

Many times, we want to know and understand. It is part of our superior creative ability. It separates us from lower forms of life that tend to accept events as they come. There is within us this insatiable need to understand. On the other hand, we seem to draw some degree of solace from our very quest to know why. No matter how painful the quest, we will still search through the rubbish of broken dreams, broken promises, and twisted childhood issues looking for clues.

We ambitiously pursue these clues because we believe there is a reward for the discovery. This emotional autopsy often takes us through the bowels of human attitudes and dysfunctional behavior. We don't have to necessarily erase the cause of our pain; we mainly just want to find some reason or justification for the pain and discomfort.

*And Jacob was left alone; and there wrestled a*
*man with him until the breaking of the day.*
Genesis 32:24

Like Jacob, all of us know what it means to be left alone. Whether through death, desertion, or even disagreement, we have all been left alone at times. We are sometimes disillusioned when we find out how easily people will leave us. Generally they leave us when we think that we *need them.* For some strange reason, human beings love to clamor around the successful more than around the struggling. They love the accomplished, but they flee the aspiring.

This may be difficult, but it is all part of God's "scholastic-achievement program" for strong believers. He is determined to strip us of our strong tendency to be dependent on others, thereby teaching us self-reliance and God-reliance. Thus the struggle truly begins not when men surround us, but rather when they forsake us. It is then that we begin to discover our own identity and self-worth!

90

It is unrealistic to expect no pain when there is disappointment or rejection. No matter how spiritual we may be, when covenants are broken and trust is betrayed, even the most stoic person will wince at the pain!

## WE NEED FEELINGS

We went through a phase once when we thought real faith meant having no feelings. Now I believe that life without feelings is like a riverbed without water. The water is what makes the river a place of activity and life. You don't want to destroy the water, but you do need to control it. Feelings that are out of control are like the floodwaters of a river. The gushing currents of boisterous waters over their banks can bring death and destruction. They must be held at bay by restrictions and limitations. Although we don't want to be controlled by feelings, we must have access to our emotions. We need to allow ourselves the pleasure and pain of life.

Emotional pain is to the spirit what physical pain is to the body. Pain warns us that something is out of order and may require attention. Pain warns us that something in our body is not healed. In the same way, when pain fills our heart, we know that we have an area where healing or restoration is needed. We dare not ignore these signals, and neither dare we let them control us.

Above all, we need to allow the Spirit of God to counsel us and guide us through the challenges of realignment when upheavals occur in our lives. Even the finest limousine requires a regular schedule of tune-ups or realignments. Minor adjustments increase performance and productivity.

It is important to understand the difference between minor and major adjustments. The removal of a person from our lives is painful, but it is not a major adjustment. Whether you realize it or not, people are being born and dying every day. They are coming and going, marrying and divorcing, falling in love and falling out of love. You can survive the loss of people, *but you can't survive without God*! He is the force that allows you to overcome when people have taken you under. His grace enables you to overcome!

## DECIDE TO KEEP GOING

Like a child who has fallen from his bicycle needs to find a place out of the view of his peers where he can honestly say, "Ouch! That hurt more than I showed in front of other people," we too need a private place of honesty. We need to be honest with ourselves. We need a place where we can sit down, reflect, and mourn. However, we must be careful not to mourn over the past longer than necessary. After the funeral, there is always a burial. The burial separates the survivor from the deceased, and it is as far as we can go. So you must come to a place of separation and decide to live on.

> *And the Lord said unto Samuel, How long wilt thou mourn for Saul, seeing I have reject-ed him from reigning over Israel? fill thine horn with oil, and go, I will send thee to Jesse*

*the Bethlehemite: for I have provided Me a*
*king among his sons.* 1 Samuel 16:1

In spite of the pain and distaste of adversity, it is impossible not to notice that *each adverse event leaves sweet nectar behind*, which, in turn, can produce its own rich honey in the character of the survivor. It is this bittersweet honey that allows us to enrich the lives of others through our experiences and testimonies. There is absolutely no substitute for the syrupy nectar of human experiences. It is these experiences that season the future relationships God has in store for us.

Unfortunately, many people leave their situation bitter and not better. Be careful to bring the richness of the experience to the hurting, not the unresolved bitterness. This kind of bitterness is a sign that the healing process in you is not over and, therefore, is not ready to be shared. When we have gone through the full cycle of survival, the situations and experiences in our lives will produce no pain, only peace.

*And He arose, and rebuked the wind, and said*
*unto the sea, Peace, be still. And the wind*
*ceased, and there was a great calm.* Mark 4:39

Have you allowed God to stand in the bow of your ship and speak peace to the thing that once terrified you? We can only benefit from resolved issues. The great tragedy is that most of us keep our pain active. Consequently, our power is never activated because our past remains unresolved. If we want to see God's power come from the pain of an experience, we must allow the process of healing to take us far beyond bitterness into a resolution that releases us from the prison and sets us free.

God's healing process makes us free to taste life again, free to trust again, and free to live without the restrictive force of threatening fears. Someone may say, "I don't want to trust again." That is only because you are not healed. To never trust again is to live on the pinnacle of a tower. You are safe from life's threatening grasp, but you are so detached from life that you soon lose consciousness of people, places, dates, and events. You become locked into a time warp. You always talk about the past *because you stopped living years ago.* Listen to your speech. You discuss the past as if it were the present because *the past has stolen the present* right out of your hand! In the name of Jesus, get it back!

## CELEBRATE NOW!

Celebration is in order. Yes, it is time to celebrate—regardless of whether you've lost a marriage, a partnership, or a personal friend. Celebration is in order because you were split from your Siamese twin and you are not dead. You are still alive! (Or at least you will be the moment you *decide* to be.) Are you ready to live, or do you still need to subject all your friends to a history class? Will you continue your incessant raging and blubbering about that which no one can change—the past?

Step into the present. Your friends will celebrate—and so will your own mind! It has been locked down, tightly tied to dead issues, and it wants to be creative and inspired again! Could it be possible that there are still those around you who want to be a part of your life, now that you have chosen to stop dwelling among the dead and in the tombs?

Perhaps I have been hard on you, but I am only trying to jump-start your heart and put you back into the presence of a real experience, far from the dank, dark valley of regret and remorse. It is easy to unconsciously live in an euphoric, almost historical mirage that causes current opportunities to evade you.

## ARE YOU ALONE?

All too often, our thoughts and conversations reveal that we wrestle with characters who have moved on and events that don't really matter. The people who surround us are kept on hold while we invest massive amounts of attention to areas of the past that are dead and possess no ability to reward. It is like slow dancing alone, or singing harmony when there is no melody. There is something missing that causes our presentation to lose its luster. Stop the music! Your partner is gone and you are waiting by yourself!

I think that the greatest of all depressions comes when we live and gather our successes just to prove something *to someone who isn't even looking*. The problem is we can't really appreciate our successes because they are done *by us* but not *for us*. They are done in the name of a person, place, or thing that has moved on, leaving us trapped in a time warp, wondering why we are not fulfilled by our job, ministry, or good fortune.

God did most of His work on creation with no one around to applaud His accomplishments. So He praised Himself. He said, "It was good!" Have you stopped to appreciate what God has allowed you to accomplish, or have you been too busy trying to make an impression on someone? No one paints for the blind or sings for the deaf. Their level of appreciation is hindered by their physical limitations. Although they may be fine connoisseurs in some other arena, they will never appreciate what they can't detect.

Let's clap and cheer for the people whose absence teaches us the gift of being alone. Somewhere beyond loneliness there is contentment, and contentment is born out of necessity. It springs up in the hum of the heart that lives in an empty house, and in the smirk and smile that comes on the face of a person who has amused himself with his own thoughts.

## PAT YOURSELF ON THE BACK

Have you reached that place in life where you enjoy your own company? Have you taken the time to enjoy your own personhood? Have you massaged lotion into your own skin, or set the dinner table for yourself? Drive yourself to the mall and spend an afternoon picking out a gift for yourself. These self-affirming ministries can never be given to you by someone else. When other people give it, it reflects their opinion about you. When they leave, you may feel worthless and insignificant. But when you speak comfort and blessings to yourself, it reflects your own opinion about yourself. The best scenario is to enjoy both kinds of affirmation.

## YOU ARE WALKING OUT A PLAN

There are three reasons to give yourself a standing ovation. The first is the fact that your steps are carefully observed and arranged by God Himself. They are designed to achieve a special purpose in your life. He brings people in and out of your life, yet you are blessed going in and going out (see Deut. 28:6). That is to say, your blessing has not and never will be predicated upon the action of another. The Bible says, "If God be for us, who can be against us?" (Rom. 8:31b) So you must rejoice because you are in step with the beat of Heaven and the purposes of God.

## YOU ARE A PERSON OF PURPOSE

Second, you ought to rejoice because you are pursuing a goal that defies human manipulation. Your blessing rests in accomplishing the will of God. Jesus went to Samaria in John 4 to minister to a hostile, religiously indifferent woman who initially had little appreciation for Him. Yet, He was nourished even by her defensive demeanor because He clearly understood that His purpose for being there was greater than the need of any one woman. Her comments lost their meaning when He weighed them against His purpose. He knew that her struggle to understand and affirm Him was of little consequence because He had a mission, yet He knew she was a part of the plan. He wasn't there to pass the time away. He was there to provoke destiny!

97

## You Have the Power

It is wonderful to have a plan, but that means nothing if you have no power to perform the plan and accomplish the purpose. God sends people in and out of your life to exercise your faith and develop your character. When they are gone, they leave you with the enriched reality that your God is with you to deliver you wherever you go! Moses died and left Joshua in charge, but God told him, "As I was with Moses, so I will be with thee" (Josh. 1:5b). Joshua never would have learned that while Moses was there. You learn this kind of thing when "Moses" is gone. Power is developed in the absence of human assistance. Then we can test the limits of our resourcefulness and the magnitude of the favor of God.

## We Can Do It!

As we go further, you may want to reevaluate who your real friends are. You see more clearly that the people who treated you the worst were actually preparing you for the best. They stripped from you the cumbersome weights and entanglements that hindered the birth of inner resilience. Yes, such friends leave us feeling naked and even vulnerable, but it is through those feelings that we begin to adapt and see our survival instincts peak. There is within the most timid person—beneath that soft, flaccid demeanor—a God-given strength that supercedes any weakness he appeared to have. The Bible puts it this way: "I can do all things through Christ which strengtheneth me" (Phil. 4:13)!

Greater still is the fact that we gain great direction through *rejection*. Rejection helps us focus on new horizons without the hindrances of wondering, "What if?" Buried deep within the broken heart is a vital need to *release and resolve*. Although we feel pain when we fail at any task, there is a sweet resolve that delivers us from the cold clutches of uncertainty. If we had not been through some degree of rejection, we would have never been selected by God. *Do you realize that God chooses people that others reject?!* From a rejected son like David to a nearly murdered son like Joseph, God gathers the castaways of men and recycles them for Kingdom building.

What frustration exists in the lives of people who want to be used of God, but who cannot endure rejection from men. I admit I haven't always possessed the personality profile that calloused me and offered some protection from the backlash of public opinion. This ability to endure is similar to having a taste for steak tartare—it must be acquired! If you want to be tenacious, you must be able to walk in the light of God's selection rather than dwell in the darkness of people's rejection. These critics are usually just a part of God's purpose in your life.

Focus is everything in ministry. If your attention is distracted by the constant thirst of other people, or if you are always trying to win people over, you will never be able to minister to the Lord—not if you are trying to win people. It seems almost as though He orchestrates your rejections to keep you from idolatry. We can easily make idols out of other people. However, God is too wise to build a house that is divided against itself. Against this rough canvas of rejection and the pain it produces, God paints the greatest sunrise the world has ever seen!

## IT'S ALL FOR OUR GOOD

> *Jesus saith unto them, Did ye never read in the scriptures, The stone which the builders reject-ed, the same is become the head of the corner: this is the Lord's doing, and it is marvellous in our eyes?* Matthew 21:42

Jesus concluded that the rejections of men He experi-enced were the doings of the Lord! As Joseph so aptly put it, "...Ye thought evil against me; but God meant it unto good" (Gen. 50:20a). The Lord orchestrates what the enemy does and makes it accomplish His purpose in your life. This is the Lord's doing! How many times have "evil" things happened in your life that later you realized were necessary? If I hadn't faced trials like these, I know that I wouldn't have been ready for the blessings I now enjoy.

In the hands of God, even our most painful circum-stances become marvelous in our eyes! When we see how perfectly God has constructed His plan, we can laugh in the face of failure. However, *rejection is only marvelous in the eyes of someone whose heart has wholly trusted in the Lord*! Have you wholly trusted in the Lord, or are you grieving over something that someone has done—as though you have no God to direct it and no grace to cor-rect it?

This is an important question because it challenges the perspectives you have chosen to take for your life. The statement, "It is marvelous in our eyes" simply means that from our perspective, the worst things look good! That is what you need faith to do! Faith is not needed just to remove problems; it is also needed to *endure* problems that seem immovable. Rest assured that even if God didn't move it, He is able! If your able God chose to stand passively by and watch someone come whose actions left you in pain, you still must trust in His sovereign grace and immutable character. He works for your good. Someone wrote a song that said, "If life hands you a lemon, just make lemonade." That's cute, but the truth is, if you walk with God, He will do the squeezing and the mixing that turns lemons into lemonade!

## PUT YOUR SEAT BELT ON

Normally, anytime there is a crash, there is an injury. If one person collides with another, they generally damage everything associated with them. In the same way, a crashing relationship affects everyone associated with it, whether it is in a corporate office, a ministry, or a family. That jarring and shaking does varying degrees of damage to everyone involved. Whether we like to admit it or not, we are affected by the actions of others to various degrees. The amount of the effect, though, depends on the nature of the relationship.

What is important is the fact that we don't have to die in the crashes and collisions of life. We must learn to live life with a seat belt in place, even though it is annoying to wear. Similarly, we need spiritual and emotional seat belts as well. We don't need the kind that harness us in and make us live like a mannequin; rather, we need the kind that are invisible, but greatly appreciated in a crash.

Inner assurance is the seat belt that stops you from going through the roof when you are rejected. It is inner assurance that holds you in place. It is the assurance that God is in control and that what He has determined no one can disallow! If He said He was going to bless you, then disregard the mess and believe a God who cannot lie. The rubbish can be cleared and the bruises can be healed. Just be sure that when the smoke clears, you are still standing. You are too important to the purpose of God to be destroyed by a situation that is only meant to give you character and direction. No matter how painful, devastated, or disappointed you may feel, you are still here. Praise God, for He will use the cornerstone developed through rejections and failed relationships to perfect what He has prepared!

Lift your voice above the screaming sirens and alarms of men whose hearts have panicked! Lift your eyes above the billowing smoke and spiraling emotions. Pull yourself up—it could have killed you, but it didn't. Announce to yourself, "I am alive. I can laugh. I can cry, and by God's grace, I can survive!"

# *C*hapter 8

## Help! My New Heart Is Living in an Old Body!

As we move onward, let's make the gradual transition from outer relationships to inward revelation. It isn't an easy step, but it is vital to our development. Eventually we learn to focus on Christ.

I remember, in my early days as a new Christian, that *I tried to become what I thought all the other Christians were.* I didn't understand that my goal should have been to achieve God's purpose for my life. I was young and so impressionable. Secretly suffering from low self-esteem, I thought that the Christians around me had mastered a level of holiness that seemed to evade me. I groaned in the night; I cried out to God to create in me a robotlike piety that would satisfy what I thought was required of me. I deeply admired those virtuous "faith heroes" whose flowery testimonies loftily hung around the ceiling like steam gathering above a shower. They seemed so changed, so sure, and so stable! I admired their standards and their purity, and I earnestly prayed, *Make me better, Lord!*

I don't think I have changed that prayer, but I have changed the *motivation* behind it. Suddenly, I began to realize that God knew me and loved me as I was, although I had never been taught about perfect love. I had always been surrounded by a love that was based upon performance. So I thought God's love was doled out according to a merit system. If I did well today, God loved me. However, if I failed, He did not love me. What a roller-coaster ride! I didn't know from moment to moment whether I was accepted in the beloved, or not!

I viewed my friends as paragons, or ultimate examples of what I should be, and I attacked my carnality with brutality. I didn't realize that everything that is born has to grow and develop to maturity. I was expecting an immediate, powerful, all-inclusive metamorphosis that would transform me into a new creature of perfection. Granted, I had never realized this goal, but I was also sure it was possible, and that this perfect creature must be much better than I. Surely God was waiting on him to come forth so He could *really* love me.

## FROM CHILD TO ADULT

Why did God bring this miraculous new creature so easily into the lives of some people when it seemed so far removed from others (like me)? I didn't realize that the "new man" starts out as a child, a child that has to grow into the mature character and nature of the Lord. No one shared with me that they had experienced struggles before they obtained victories. No one told me that wars come before success.

I was saved, but I was miserable. My misery deepened as I tried to measure up to others and answer all the concerns that plagued my heart. I was in a desperate search before anyone else realized that I wasn't always on the mountaintop like those around me seemed to be. I felt ashamed. My heart cried out, *What must I do to be perfected in the Lord?*

It is a tormenting experience for us to try to accomplish *through ourselves* what only God and maturity can accomplish in time. No matter how much my young son wants to wear my clothes, he cannot wear them today because he isn't old enough or developed enough to wear them. Yet, *there is absolutely nothing wrong with him.* He is as big as he should be for his age. Sometimes we are expected to be further along than we should be for the age we are in God!

## Let God Mature You

It is important for us to let God mature us—without our self-help efforts to impress others with a false sense of piety. That kind of do-it-yourself righteousness and religion keeps us from being naked before God and from being comfortable with our own level of growth. Yes, I want to be all that God wants me to be. But while I am developing at the rate He has chosen, I will certainly thank Him for His rich grace and bountiful mercy along the way. This is the divine mercy that lets us mature naturally.

Many Christians struggle to produce a *premature change* when God-ordained change can only be accomplished according to His time. We cannot expect to change the flesh. It will not respond to therapy. God intends for us to grow spiritually while we live in our vile, corrupt flesh. It is His will that our treasure be displayed in a cabinet of putrid, unregenerated flesh—openly displaying the strange dichotomy between the temporal and the eternal.

It is amazing that God would put so much in so little. The true wonder of His glory is painted on the dark canvas of our old personhood. What a glorious backdrop our weakness makes for His strength! This backdrop is absolutely crucial. "Paul's thorn," the glaring symbol of human weakness contrasted with God's greatness, was given as a humbling reminder to the great apostle to insure him against arrogance and pride (see 2 Cor. 12:7).

Paul wanted the thorn removed, but God wanted it "endured." Many times we, like Paul, *ask God to remove what He wants us to endure.* There is a great deal of power released through the friction of the holy graces of God grating against the dry, gritty surface of human incapacities and limitations. We sharpen our testimonies whenever we press His glory against our struggles. Although Paul sought diligently for the removal of his thorn, the reality is that Paul's thorn was as much in God's plan for the apostle's life as any other trial, victory, or accomplishment in ministry.

God's sovereignty allocates the grace necessary for us to know Him in "the fellowship of His sufferings" (see

Phil. 3:10). What suffering? Well, we are not being asked (at this time, anyway) to lay down our physical lives for the gospel. No one has stripped the clothes from our over-weight backsides and beaten our pampered, lotion-soft-ened skin. Our sunglass-covered eyes haven't been gouged out of their sockets. No, it is enough for now that we are asked to live in an unchanged body!

The problem is that while we are changed in our spirit by the new birth, our old corruptible body and fleshly desires are not. They are spirit-controlled, but not spirit-destroyed! The Holy Spirit is living with us in a stinking clay pot—a putrid, decaying, clay-covered, vile body. Its stench is so bad that we must continually wash and perfume it just to endure living there ourselves. Yet God Himself, the epitome of purity, has forsaken the rich, robust pavilions of His holy domain to live in a fail-ing, decaying, deteriorating, collapsing, and corroding shell.

## GOD INHABITS AN OLD HOUSE

Within our decaying shells, we constantly peel away, by faith, the lusts and jealousies that adorn the walls of our hearts. If the angels were to stroll through the earth with the Creator and ask, "Which house is Yours?" He would pass by all the mansions and cathedrals, all the temples and castles. Unashamedly, He would point at you and me and say, "That house is Mine!" Imagine the shock and disdain of the heavenly host to think that the God whose face they fan with their wings would choose to live in such a shack and shanty! We know where our greatest conflict lies. We who blunder and stumble in our

humanity, we who stagger through our frail existence—
we continually wrestle with the knowledge that *our God
has put so much in so little*!

Yes, it is true: Despite all our washing and painting,
all our grooming and exercising, this old house is still
falling apart! We train it and teach it. We buy books and
tapes, and we desperately try to convince it to at least
think differently. But like a squeaky hinge on a swollen
door, the results of our efforts, at best, come slowly. There
is no doubt that we have been saved, and *there is no
doubt that the house is haunted.* The Holy Ghost Himself
resides beneath this sagging roof. (Although the tenant is
prestigious, the accommodations are still substandard.)

This divine occupation is not an act of a desperate
guest who, having no place else to stay, chose this impoverished site as a temporary place to "ride out" the storm
of some deplorable situation. No, God Himself has—of
His own free will and predetermined purpose—put us in
the embarrassing situation of entertaining a Guest whose
lofty stature so far exceeds us that we hardly know how
to serve Him!

The very best of us camouflage the very worst in us
with religious colloquialisms that reduce Christianity to
more of an act than an attitude. Even the most pious
among us—while in the quiet booth of some confessional
or kneeling in solitude at the edge of our beds—must
murmur our confession before God: *We have earnestly
pursued a place in You that we have not attained.*

Our struggle continues to feed the ravenous appetite of our holy Guest, whose divine hunger requires us to perpetually feed Him a sacrificial life. He daily consumes, and continually requires, that which we alone know God wants from us. Paul battled to bring into submission the hidden things in his life that could bring destruction. Perhaps they were putrid thoughts, or vain imaginations, or pride; but whatever they were, he declared war on them if they resisted change. He says, in essence, that as he waits for the change, he keeps his body in chains, beating back the forces of evil.

> *But I keep under my body, and bring it into subjection: lest that by any means, when I have preached to others, I myself should be a castaway.* 1 Corinthians 9:27

This is the struggle of the same man who wrote the majority of the New Testament! With a testimony like this, I pay very little attention to those among us who feel obligated to impress us with the ludicrous idea that they have already attained what is meant to be a lifelong pursuit. The renewal of the old man is a daily exercise of the heart. It progressively strengthens the character day by day, not overnight!

I remember some of those wonderful gospel songs that we used to sing that said, "I looked at my hands and my hands looked new, I looked at my feet and they did too…." Those are wonderful lyrics, but they are completely erroneous. They sounded exciting, but they were tragically misleading. If you want to know the truth, if you had a bunion on your foot *before* you got saved, and you were to take your shoes off and check it *after* you got saved, it would still be holding on!

## INSIDE THAT OLD HOUSE

So the bad news is that the old house is still a death trap; it's still infested with rodents. A legion of thoughts and pesky memories crawl around in our heads like roaches that come out in the night and boldly parade around the house. Add to this pestilence an occasional groaning in the dungeon, and you will have a picturesque view of the inner workings of a Christian! That should not negate our joy, though; it merely confesses our struggles.

What do I mean by "groaning"? The occasional groaning you hear is not demonic. Rather, it is a painful groan that pierces our nights like the whelping cry of a wounded animal. We have not been taught about the crying of the Spirit, but I tell you that the Holy Spirit can be grieved. He has the capacity and ability to groan within us until His groaning emerges as conviction in the heart of the humble. Yes, it is bad news, but the Guest we entertain desires more for us than what we have in us! He enjoys neither the house nor the clothing we offer Him. He just suffers it like a lover suffers adversity to be in the company of the one he loves.

The good news is that the bad news won't last long! Jesus said, "...every city or house divided against itself shall not stand" (Mt. 12:25). Ever since we were saved, there has been a division in the house. Eventually the old house will have to yield to the new one! Yes, we are constantly renovating through the Word of God, but the truth is that God will eventually *recycle* what you and I have been trying to *renovate*! It is then that the groaning of the regenerated spirit within us will transform into sheer glory!

> For we know that if our earthly house of this tabernacle were dissolved, we have a building of God, an house not made with hands, eternal in the heavens. For in this we groan, earnestly desiring to be clothed upon with our house which is from heaven: if so be that being clothed we shall not be found naked. For we that are in this tabernacle do groan, being burdened: not for that we would be unclothed, but clothed upon, that mortality might be swallowed up of life. Now He that hath wrought us for the selfsame thing is God, who also hath given unto us the earnest of the Spirit.
> 2 Corinthians 5:1-5

## AN INTERNAL CONFLICT

Christianity means conflict. At the least, if it doesn't mean conflict, it certainly *creates* conflict! The question is, why are we so silent? Why do we seldom hear anyone say that "living holy" isn't natural? *It isn't natural—it is spiritual!* Unless we walk consistently in the spirit, living holy is difficult. No, it is impossible! It isn't natural to "do good to them that hate you" (see Mt. 5:44). You don't see one dog steal another one's bone and then see the betrayed dog wag his tail in happiness! No, forgiveness isn't natural.

Without God it cannot be done! Being a Christian means that one part of you is constantly wanting to do the right thing while the other part of you is desperately campaigning for you to walk in your old habits. We often talk about how God saved us from sin. I agree. I am grateful for the terribly wicked things that He saved me from. Because I was saved, I didn't commit those wicked sins, but I would have had He not set up a protest in my heart! He brought my trembling soul to His bleeding side and cleansed my very imaginations, intentions, and ambitions! Yes, the Christian life is a life of conflict, and I thank God that He groans and protests my sinful behavior. It is because He challenges my proclivities that growth begins!

*Now there was long war between the house of Saul and the house of David: but David waxed stronger and stronger, and the house of Saul waxed weaker and weaker.* 2 Samuel 3:1

Transformation is a process! It takes faith and patience to see the results that bring out the true nature of Christ in any of us. It is when we strip away the facade of the superficial and ask God to bring about the supernatural that we experience the real power of God. God wants to transport us from the superficial to the supernatural!

## WHO WAS MORE A KING?

Saul was anointed by God to be king. He was more moral than David in that he didn't struggle in some of the areas that plagued David. His weakness wasn't outward; it was inward. Saul looked like a king, whereas David looked like an underage juvenile delinquent who should have been home taking care of the flocks. But David wasn't in the palace; he was out there with the men, fighting the giants and bringing about change. Saul's armor shined in the noonday sun. David had no armor. He fought naked, free from the entanglements of trying to be impressive. He was not ashamed. Even his weapon looked substandard; it was just an old, ragged, shepherd's slingshot.

Although David's weapon was outwardly substandard, it was nevertheless lethal; it led to the destruction of the giant. We can never destroy our enemy with the superficial armor of a pious king. We don't need the superficial. We need the supernatural! David's naked, transparent demeanor was so translucent that he often seems extremely vulnerable. He seems almost naive at times. When he worships, he does it with holy abandonment. When he lusts, he does it to obsessive dimensions. You would almost think he was unfit, except that when he repents, there is something so powerful in his prayer that even his most adamant critic must admire his openness with God!

> Have mercy upon me, O God, according to Thy
> lovingkindness: according unto the multitude
> of Thy tender mercies blot out my transgres-
> sions. Wash me thoroughly from mine iniquity,
> and cleanse me from my sin. For I acknowl-
> edge my transgressions: and my sin is ever
> before me. Against Thee, Thee only, have I
> sinned, and done this evil in Thy sight: that
> Thou mightest be justified when Thou speak-
> est, and be clear when Thou judgest. Behold, I

*was shapen in iniquity; and in sin did my
mother conceive me. Behold, Thou desirest
truth in the inward parts: and in the hidden
part Thou shalt make me to know wisdom.
Purge me with hyssop, and I shall be clean:
wash me, and I shall be whiter than snow.
Make me to hear joy and gladness; that the
bones which Thou hast broken may rejoice.
Hide Thy face from my sins, and blot out all
mine iniquities. Create in me a clean heart, O
God; and renew a right spirit within me. Cast
me not away from Thy presence; and take not
Thy Holy Spirit from me. Restore unto me the
joy of Thy salvation; and uphold me with Thy
free spirit. Then will I teach transgressors Thy
ways; and sinners shall be converted unto
Thee. Deliver me from bloodguiltiness, O God,
Thou God of my salvation: and my tongue
shall sing aloud of Thy righteousness.*
Psalm 51:1-14

What a sharp contrast there is between David and
King Saul, whose stately demeanor and pompous gait
didn't stop him from being an incredible deceiver. Even
when he was face-to-face with Samuel the prophet, Saul
lied at a time he should have repented! The problem with
Saul and people like him is that they are more interested
in their *image* than they are concerned about being
immaculate in their hearts.

While Saul stood arrayed in his kingly attire, boast-
ing of his conquest over an enemy king and lying about
his real struggles, the heathen king whom Saul had been

commanded to kill was still alive. The sheep that he had been ordered to destroy were still bleating in the valley. God did not destroy Saul for not killing what he should have killed; that wasn't the biggest problem. God can work with weakness; in fact, His strength is made perfect in our human weakness (see 2 Cor. 12:9). The central problem was that Saul's *deceitfulness* had become a breach too wide to bridge. David might have been weak, and struggled with moral issues, but at least *he was naked before God*!

> *And Saul said, They have brought them from the Amalekites: for the people spared the best of the sheep and of the oxen, to sacrifice unto the Lord thy God; and the rest we have utterly destroyed. Then Samuel said unto Saul, Stay, and I will tell thee what the Lord hath said to me this night. And he said unto him, Say on. And Samuel said, When thou wast little in thine own sight, wast thou not made the head of the tribes of Israel, and the Lord anointed thee king over Israel? And the Lord sent thee on a journey, and said, Go and utterly destroy the sinners the Amalekites, and fight against them until they be consumed. Wherefore then didst thou not obey the voice of the Lord, but didst fly upon the spoil, and didst evil in the sight of the Lord? And Saul said unto Samuel, Yea, I have obeyed the voice of the Lord, and have gone the way which the Lord sent me, and have brought Agag the king of Amalek, and have utterly destroyed the Amalekites. But*

*the people took of the spoil, sheep and oxen,*
*the chief of the things which should have been*
*utterly destroyed, to sacrifice unto the Lord thy*
*God in Gilgal. And Samuel said, Hath the Lord*
*as great delight in burnt offerings and sacri-*
*fices, as in obeying the voice of the Lord?*
*Behold, to obey is better than sacrifice, and to*
*hearken than the fat of rams. For rebellion is as*
*the sin of witchcraft, and stubbornness is as*
*iniquity and idolatry. Because thou hast reject-*
*ed the word of the Lord, He hath also rejected*
*thee from being king. And Saul said unto*
*Samuel, I have sinned: for I have transgressed*
*the commandment of the Lord, and thy words:*
*because I feared the people, and obeyed their*
*voice. 1 Samuel 15:15-24*

Saul represents that part of all of us that must be overthrown. It is *the leadership of Saul in us* that must be renounced if we are to go beyond the superficial and fulfill our destiny in the supernatural. God knows who we are. He can deliver us from ourselves, but we must be honest enough to say, *This is all You have to work with, God. What can You do with what I have presented?* Misrepresentation will not be tolerated! There must be an open confession that enables God's grace to be allocated to your need.

## BE HONEST!

Now hear this, you who would allow the spirit of Saul to reign in your life: The house of Saul represents those fleshly areas that we war against. These are areas that hide in religious clothes but do not worship God in honesty—not perfection, just honesty. Saul was perhaps "more moral" than David, but David was by far "more honest." Consequently, the house of Saul grew weaker and weaker and the house of David grew stronger and stronger!

There is a gradual and perpetual transference of authority as we walk with God. We move from the Saul-like rule of superficial religion to a Davidic anointing based on honesty and transparency. Like a chick pecking through its shell, we press through our concerns and over other people's opinions, and break into the light to know God in a more definitive way!

"My little children, of whom I travail in birth again until Christ be formed in you" (Gal. 4:19). Only God knows the process it will take for the Christ who saved you to be formed in you. He is taking each of us to that place where the child begins to bear a greater resemblance to his Father. Be assured that this only occurs at the end of travailing prayer and openness of heart, as we confess and forsake every trace of Saul's rule in our lives.

# $\mathcal{C}$hapter 9

## NO ADDITIVES: THE BLOOD ALONE

The blood is the only element in the body that reaches, affects, and fuels all other parts of the body. This rich, reddish-purple elixer flows silently through the cardiovascular system like high-powered cars moving on interstate highways. It carries the cargo of much-needed oxygen molecules and nutrients that are necessary to sustain life in every cell of the body. If the blood is restricted long enough from any member of the body, that member will internally asphyxiate, and begin to change colors. Its asphyxiated cells can quickly die—even without an external assailant—for their affliction is the result of *internal deprivation*.

Every member, every limb and organ in the human body, needs the blood. Along with its culinary duty of delivering soluble dietary contents throughout the body, our blood has the additional responsibility of functioning as a paramedic. Its white blood cells stand ready to attack adverse intruders in the form of bacteria or foreign cells, or any other foreign substance that may try to disrupt the vitality of the body. The white blood cells are the body's "militia." These cells are uniquely equipped to fight off attacking bacteria and expel it from the body—stripping it of its power and robbing it of its spoils.

> *For as we have many members in one body,*
> *and all members have not the same office: so*
> *we, being many, are one body in Christ, and*
> *every one members one of another.*
> Romans 12:4-5

The physical body echoes and illustrates the power of the blood in the Church, the mystical Body of Christ. Every member of the Body of Christ—regardless of morality, maturity, or position—needs the life-giving blood of Jesus. Without the blood, we cease to have the proof of our sonship. Isn't the blood what physicians test to determine and verify who is the father of a child? Without the blood, we are only bastard sons camouflaged as real sons. Without His blood, we are pseudo-heirs trying to receive the promises reserved for the legitimate sons of God!

## WE STILL NEED THE BLOOD!

We did not need the blood only for when we cried out to the Lord to come into our hearts by faith and rescue us from impending danger. On the contrary, we *still need that same blood today*. All our strength and nourishment and every promise and miracle must flow to us *through the blood*. Satan hates the blood—not only because it redeemed us, but also because it continues to give us life from day to day!

> *How much more shall the blood of Christ, who through the eternal Spirit offered Himself without spot to God, purge your conscience from dead works to serve the living God? And for this cause He is the mediator of the new testament, that by means of death, for the redemption of the transgressions that were under the first testament, they which are called might receive the promise of eternal inheritance.*
> Hebrews 9:14-15

We have lost our teaching of the blood in this age of Pentecostalism (of which I am adamantly a part). We have learned about the Spirit of God, but we failed to teach believers about the blood. Consequently, we have produced a generation of believers who are empowered by the Spirit but do not feel forgiven! They are empowered, yet they are insecure. They are operating in the gifts, but living in guilt!

Oh, hear me today! The blood must be preached. Without it we have no life. No, the preaching of the blood will not weaken the Church! To the contrary, it will relieve us of a prepaid debt. Why are we wasting the power of God on the problems of our past? *The blood has already totally destroyed the past bondages that held us down!* It was through the eternal Spirit of God that Jesus was able to offer up His blood. The Spirit always refers us back to the blood. *There can be no Pentecost where there is no Passover!*

## THE BLOOD IS FOR ALL

There is a devilish prejudice in the Church that denies the blood to its uncomely members. If a person has a failure in an area we relate to because we have a similar weakness, we immediately praise God for the blood that cleanses us from all unrighteousness. If they are unfortunate enough to fail where we are very strong, then *we condemn them*. We tie a string around those members to mark them, and we deny them the blood.

The spirit of Cain is loose in the Church! We have spilled our brother's blood because he is different, because his skin or his sin is different from ours. Untie them right now, in the name of the Lord, and restore to them the opportunity to experience the life that only comes to the flesh through the blood. *Without the blood all flesh dies*—black, white, rich, poor, homosexual, heterosexual, drug addict, or alcoholic. Without the blood of Christ to save it and the Holy Spirit to empower it, no flesh can be saved.

But by the blood of the Lamb, any man, regardless of his failures or past sin, can come equally and unashamedly to the foot of the cross and allow the drops of Jesus' blood to invigorate the soul that sin has lacerated and destroyed. We will never experience massive revival until we allow *all sinners* to come to the fountain filled with blood, drawn from Emmanuel's veins!

Have you ever been guilty of having a condescending attitude about another person's weakness? I am ashamed to admit it, but I have. How can we dare to think we can access the soul-cleansing blood that delivers us from the cesspool of our secret sins, and then look down on another member of Christ's Body in disdain? *How can we forbid them access* to the only answer to the massive problems that consume our generation?

## The Antidote

The blood of Christ is God's antidote to the plague of sin that has attacked the world and, yes, even the Body of Christ! We may have different symptoms, just as a flu virus may produce different symptoms in different people, but we all suffer from a fatal infection of sin! Sin has affected us differently according to our backgrounds and circumstances, but regardless of the symptoms, it is still the same disease. There is but one cure: the blood. "Come to the fountain so full and free. Cast your poor soul at the Savior's feet. Come in today and be made complete. Glory to His name!" ("Down at the Cross," Elisha A. Hoffman, 1878).

> *Unto Adam also and to his wife did the Lord
> God make coats of skins, and clothed them.*
> Genesis 3:21

We have presented no solution to the tragedies of life that afflict our members. We have offered them no balm for the injuries that come from inner flaws and failure. Because we have offered no provision for the sons and daughters who *fall*, many of our Adams and our Eves are hiding in the bushes. Our fallen brethren hear our message, but they cannot come out to a preacher or a crowd that merely points out their nakedness and has nothing in hand to cover them. We need to offer the perfect sacrifice to the sons of God as well as to the world. Adam was God's son. He was fallen and he was foolish, but he was the son of God!

> *Which was the son of Enos, which was the son*
> *of Seth, which was the son of Adam, which*
> *was the son of God.* Luke 3:38

The blood of Christ will even reach the falling, faltering son who hides in the bushes of our churches. He has fig leaves all around him. He is illicit and immoral. Who will walk the cool of the garden to find him? Even harder yet, who will walk the heat of the jungle to cover him? Many of us are taking the first walk to *discover the fallen*, but they have not taken the deeper walk to *cover the fallen*. How can this son stand naked and unashamed if we offer no sanctity or holiness in exchange for his failure, yet have great mercy for our own shortcomings? When God covered Adam and Eve's nakedness, *He covered what He discovered* with the bloody skins of an innocent animal, giving Himself the first sacrifice to atone for their sin.

## STANDING IN THE BLOOD-SOAKED SKINS

Before Adam could receive the covering God had provided, though, he had to disrobe himself of what he had contrived. It is in this process that many believers are trapped. We are so uncomfortable with our humanity that we are afraid to risk removing our contrived religious facade long enough for God to bring us, as the hymnist so aptly declared, "dressed in His righteousness alone, faultless to stand before the throne!" ("My Hope Is Built," Edward Mote, 1832).

Adam stripped himself before a holy God, admitted his tragic sins, and still maintained his position as a son in the presence of God. Adam and Eve realized at that moment that *the only solution for their sin was in the perfect provision of their loving God.* That same loving God now reaches out to us *as we are*, and refashions us into what we should become!

Adam stood as I do, *in the warm skins of a freshly slain sacrifice* that made it possible for him to continue to live. It was actually no more Adam who lived; rather, he was now living the life of the innocent lamb. Just as surely as the innocent lamb had taken Adam's place in death, Adam continued to live on, wrapped in the coverings of the lamb's life! Can you understand more clearly what Paul means when he says, "accepted in the beloved"? (See Ephesians 1:6.) If Adam were seen out from under the covering of those bloody skins, he could not be accepted. But because of the shedding of innocent blood, there was remission of sin for him!

We hear no further mention of blame or guilt concerning the first family as they walked away from the worst moment in the history of humanity. Why? They were wrapped and protected in the provision of God. We can find no more arguments, fault-finding, or condemnation in Scripture. I have not read where Adam blamed Eve anymore. Neither did Eve judge Adam, for they both realized that *had it not been for the blood*, neither would have been there.

We too need to have this knowledge—regardless of the differences in our specific flaws; regardless of whom we would want to blame or belittle. If the blood had failed to reach the liar, then he would be as lost as the child molester! The symptoms are different, but the disease and its prognosis are the same. The disease is sin, the wage or prognosis is death, and the antidote prescribed is the blood and the blood alone. Never forget the blood, for without it we have no good news at all!

## BECOMING HONEST AND OPEN

I can't help but wonder what would happen if we would ever love like Jesus loves. I know it seems impossible, but I believe that all of creation is waiting for the sons of God to come to themselves. Creation is yearning for us to become what we were meant to be in terms of honesty and transparency. Even the best of us have failed to completely disrobe and dislodge ourselves from the many-layered clothes of vain religiosity. However, as we peel away layer by layer, as we become more comfortable with our God and our own humanity, we become increasingly transparent. We are surprised to find that there are not nearly as many significant differences between us as we were led to believe.

Perhaps we can learn how to be as open about our failures as we are about our successes. Without that kind of honesty, we create a false image that causes others to needlessly struggle. When others hear our one-sided testimony of successes with no failure, they become discouraged. They realize that they are wrestling while we seem to "have it together." They feel that they don't qualify to receive what God has done for us because we have falsified the records and failed to tell the truth!

Adam found himself stripped of his fig leaves. He stood naked before his wife and his God. Those are two important areas. We must wrestle to achieve a level of honesty that will keep us from being estranged from the ones we are connected to. We have to love and be loved by someone to the degree that we can say, *This is who I am, and it is all that I am. Love me and be patient with me. There is no telling what I will become, but today this is who I am.*

When you find someone who can see your flaws and your underdeveloped character, *and love you in spite of it all*, you are blessed. If the only way you can love me is after I have perfected my imperfections, then you really don't love me. As I progress I will always wonder, "Do you love me for who I am?"

Many marriages seem to pass the test as long as both parties are perfect in the major areas. But when one party becomes defective in one of those major areas, the relationship is often destroyed. God was too wise to wait until you perfected the defective. He loved you while you were unlovable so you would never have to hide in the bushes again! He has loved you with an everlasting love!

## The Greatness of God's Goodness

*But God commendeth His love toward us, in that, while we were yet sinners, Christ died for us.* Romans 5:8

It sounds mushy, and to the religious zealot it may sound too loose and simplistic, but we need to remember that *it is the goodness of God that leads to repentance* (see Rom. 2:4). Repentance doesn't come because of the scare tactics and threats of raging ministers who need mercy themselves. Repentance comes because of the unfailing love of a perfect God, a God who cares for the cracked vases that others would have discarded. It is His great love that causes a decision to be made in the heart: *I must live for Him!*

There is no way that you can see Him stand with you when all others forsake you, and not want to please Him! There is no way you can weather a storm in His loving arms and not say, "I am Yours, O Lord. Such as I have I give to You." One gaze into His holiness will bring the sinner crashing to the floor on bended knees, confessing and forsaking, wrestling and controlling every issue that would have engulfed him before his wandering eye affixed itself on the manifold graces of God!

In other words, God is too good for us to experience His love and then be contented to abuse that love. *Accepting the rejected is not the weakness of the gospel; it is its strength!* No, we cannot shelter hardened criminals who are content to live as outlaws from the Word of the Lord. But there is a great deal of difference between the cold callousness of a rebellious heart and the deeply troubled heart of a transforming Christian whose whispered prayer is, "God, save me from myself." It is to the distraught heart that seeks so desperately for a place of refuge that we extend soft hands and tender words.

To the survivors of wrecked ships and damaged homes, we hold out our arms. As we do, they will come— the halt and the lame, the deaf and dumb. They will need much of the Word and much time before their marriages cease to tremble and their self-images improve. They will have flashbacks and relapses, and require intensive care. Yet we swing wide the doors of ministry and admit, at the risk of being blatantly naked, that *most of our doctors have at one time been patients*, and that many of them are still being treated. Still we say, "Come," for we are not the medicine—it is Christ who is the cure!

To the overlooked and the castaway, to the down-trodden and the wayfaring, we cry, "Come into this shelter; come out of the cold. If nowhere else, and by no one else, you are *accepted in the beloved*!"

## What About the Church?

How can we then define the Church, with its rising divorce rate and afflicted leadership? Doesn't the Church need to bathe itself in its own message? Yes, it does. But then who said the Church would not? This "dippity-doo, a little dab will do you" mentality that we preach is not scriptural at all. We need treatment every day. We have strengths and struggles. We have conflicts and conquests, conquerings and challenges. We are not a finished product. Why have we boxed ourselves in and lifted ourselves up as the epitome of sanctity? Beneath our stained glass windows and padded pews lay broken hearts and torn families, those who chose to wait in the aisle of His presence rather than die in the stables of our wretchedness!

We have no right to be blessed, in ourselves. We are neither worthy nor deserving of it. Yet He has blessed us "in spite of us." Our testimony must change. Away with the polished brass words from silver-spooned lips that suggest anonymity from failure and fear. If we tell the truth (and we seldom do), it was the *blood* that brought us here. Beneath the streaming tears of a grateful heart, through our trembling lips must emerge the birthing thoughts that Christ has done it all, and that we have nothing to boast in but His precious blood—and His blood alone!

## CHRIST ON THE CROSS

Before I close this chapter on the precious effect of His blood, I must take one final, longing look back at Calvary's bloody banks. As the eclipsed sun tucked itself behind the trembling ground, a ground still wet with the cascading blood of a loving Savior, Jesus' love was so awesome that it could only be depicted by the morbidity of His dying. Allow this country preacher, this West Virginia hillbilly, a final glimpse at the only hope his soul has of Heaven. Brush a tear from a face full of thanksgiving and look at His bruised, mutilated, and lacerated body. Look at the 33-year-old body that could have been the object of some loving lady's desire. The body that was filled with such youth and potential now hangs from the cross like a slab of unused meat. From His beaten back to His ripped torso, we see a wounded knight without armor. His garments lay crumbled on the ground, the object of the desires of His villainous guards who now gamble up their leisure moments, waiting on the death angel to flap his wings in the face of the Savior.

Ignore the ice-cream social pictures of modern artists who portray a sunning Savior, basking in divine light before an alabaster sky as He gazes listlessly and lovingly out at a dying world. Ignore their imagery of a prince clad in some magical loincloth that seems, even in the pictures, to be somehow superimposed on the body of this spiritual celebrity. When you look at this icon of grace, remove your religious glasses and you will see a sweat-drenched, trembling, bleeding offering. That crucifixion was a debauchery and degradation so horrible that it embarrassed the sun into hiding its face and made the ground tremble at the nervous sight of the King of glory. He hung dying as if He were the bastard son of Mary, not the King that He was—dying like a thief in the night! His body, twisted and mangled, was held to a tree and suspended by nails as if some Marquis de Sade-type sadist had relished torturing the innocent.

*And they stripped Him, and put on Him a scarlet robe. And when they had platted a crown of thorns, they put it upon His head, and a reed in His right hand: and they bowed the knee before Him, and mocked Him, saying, Hail, King of the Jews! And they spit upon Him, and took the reed, and smote Him on the head. And after that they had mocked Him, they took the robe off from Him, and put His own raiment on Him, and led Him away to crucify Him. And as they came out, they found a man of Cyrene, Simon by name: him they compelled to bear His cross. And when they were come unto a place called Golgotha, that is*

*to say, a place of a skull, they gave Him vine-*
*gar to drink mingled with gall: and when He*
*had tasted thereof, He would not drink. And*
*they crucified Him, and parted His garments,*
*casting lots: that it might be fulfilled which was*
*spoken by the prophet, They parted My gar-*
*ments among them, and upon My vesture did*
*they cast lots. And sitting down they watched*
*Him there.* Matthew 27:28-36

To me, Jesus Christ is the Prince of Peace. But to
them, He was the entertainment for the evening. *They*
*stripped Him completely and totally.* They humiliated
Him by placing a robe upon His nude body and a crown
upon His weary head, and then they amused themselves
with Him. When they could do no more, they stripped
Him of the robe and put His own clothes upon Him and
led Him away to the cross. At the cross, Jesus again was
stripped of His own clothes like the innocent animal in
the Book of Genesis was stripped of its coat of skin.

Likewise, *Jesus was made bare that I might be cov-*
*ered.* Climbing naked upon the cross, He lay nailed to a
tree! They then parted His garments among themselves
and watched Him, *naked and not ashamed!* They
watched until grace grew weary and mercifully draped a
curtain over the sun, allowing darkness to veil Him from
the watchful eyes of unconcerned hearts. These are the
eyes of coldhearted men, men whose eyes are still dark-
ened today lest they behold the wonder of His glory.
That is why they can't quite see what we see when we
look at Calvary!

The Savior's head is pricked with the thorns of every issue that would ever rest on my mind. His hands are nailed through for every vile thing I have ever used mine to do. His feet are nailed to the tree for every illicit, immoral place you and I have ever walked in! Sweat and blood race down His tortured frame. His oozing, gaping wounds are tormented by the abrasive bark of that old rugged cross, and are assaulted by the salty sweat of a dying man. In spite of His pain and abuse, in spite of His torment and His nudity, He was still preaching as they watched Him dying—*naked and not ashamed*!

Oh preacher, you say you've been through some things and that you've been hurt—still you must not stop preaching. Even though you have been stripped and others have beheld your nakedness, there are still some who will hear your words. Some dying thief will relate to you—if you can preach through your nudity and minister through your pain. Someone will relate to you and be saved because you stayed at your post and did what you were called to do!

## So What About the Loincloth?

Yes, the tormentors unveiled Him as if they were unmasking a painting. His nailed hands were denied the privilege of hiding Himself. He was exposed. So what about the issue of the loincloth? Where did this loincloth come from? Why is it painted on most of the pictures I see of the cross? Isn't that what hinders us now? Are we, the Body of Christ, hiding beneath a loincloth that has stifled our testimony and blocked our ability to be transparent, even with one another? There is seemingly some secret order whereby *we have not been allowed to share our struggles as well as our successes.* Our ministers are dying of loneliness because they feel obligated to maintain some false image of perfection in order to be serviceable in our society. We have no one to laugh with, no one to cry with, and no one who will sit down and share a sandwich with us. Beneath the loincloth of human expectation and excessive demands, many men and women are bleeding to death!

The greater tragedy is the fact that the loincloth represents all those things that are *humanly imposed upon us,* things that God does not require! The loincloth, regardless of how appropriate, moral, or sanctimonious it might seem, only exists in the minds of the artists who, in turn, painted what *they thought* we could stand to see. The Bible, on the other hand, says, "The Lord hath made bare His holy arm..." (Is. 52:10)!

I resent the loincloth because it is almost prophetic of what the Church, the mystical Body of Christ, has done today. We have hidden our humanity beneath the manmade cloths of religiosity. *We have covered up what God has made bare!* Now we have to face secular news reporters who are trying to expose what should have been uncovered from the beginning. We are not God! We are men—men made of clay who have the power of God. We should apologize for ever trying to pass ourselves off as anything more. *We need no loincloth; the Body of Christ was meant to be naked and not ashamed.* Like the physical body of Christ, we have been camouflaged beneath religious loincloths. Like Adam's fig leaves, our loincloth is our attempt to cover what only God can cover.

Was the body of Christ covered? Yes, but not with any man-made material. The body of Christ was meant to be covered with nothing but the blood of Christ. Anything else is vain and ineffective. The cascading blood that flowed from His gaping wounds was the dressing of the Lord. His provision for our nudity was His blood. He knew that the death angel would soon pass by, and loin-cloths do not impress him. But that angel said, "When I see the blood, I will pass over you."

I hope you have only one defense when it is your turn to go on trial. Do not submit a loincloth for evidence; it is inadmissible. But my wounded, hurting, healing, helping, giving and needing friend, when they try your case (and they surely will), open your mouth, clear your throat, and plead, *No additives; the blood alone!*

# *C*hapter 10

## HE LAID ASIDE HIS GARMENTS

*And supper being ended, the devil having now put into the heart of Judas Iscariot, Simon's son, to betray Him; Jesus knowing that the Father had given all things into His hands, and that He was come from God, and went to God; He riseth from supper, and laid aside His garments; and took a towel and girded Himself. After that He poureth water into a basin, and began to wash the disciples' feet, and to wipe them with the towel wherewith He was girded.*
John 13:2-5

Supper is over and the dishes are cleared away. Supper is also over for those of us who have had a "reality check" through the unveiling of Judas. We now realize that our ultimate purpose for gathering isn't really for fellowship. He gathers us to sharpen and prune us through our attempts at fellowship. He often uses the people with whom we worship to prune us. They become the utensils the Lord uses to perfect those whom He has called. As lavishly garnished as the table is, and as decorative as it may appear to the youthful gaze of the new Christian, it is only a matter of time before they begin the stage-by-stage unmasking and realize that the guests around the table of the Lord are bleeding.

## A Shocking Guest List

Imagine how shocked you would be to find yourself invited to a prestigious dinner party like this one. You have been so careful to respond appropriately. Now shaven and manicured, clean and perfumed, you carefully begin the laborious task of attiring yourself in an elegant, yet tasteful manner. You desperately want to make a positive impression on the Host, as well as on the guests. After arriving on time, you hasten toward the door where you are announced and then ushered into the banqueting room of your dreams.

The Host is dazzling—more splendid than your imagination could have ever concocted. In fact, He is so awesome that you scarcely notice the guests at all. As the evening wears on and the supper is presented by course, each one more exquisite than the first, you begin to focus your attention on the other guests.

As your eyes begin to warily make the rounds across the table, a bitter taste of bile begins to rise and lodge in your throat. Each guest has some sort of gross deformity beneath their gracious smile. Neither rubies nor diamonds, neither tuxedos nor tails can camouflage the scars and gaping wounds represented around the table. You are shocked that you spent all evening trying to prepare yourself to meet people who have more flaws than you have ever imagined! The only spotless splendor for the human eye to gaze upon is the Host Himself—all others are merely patients; just mutilated, torn, dilapidated, disfigured caricatures of social grace and ambiance.

> So that servant came, and shewed his lord these things. Then the master of the house being angry said to his servant, Go out quickly into the streets and lanes of the city, and bring in hither the poor, and the maimed, and the halt, and the blind. And the servant said, Lord, it is done as thou hast commanded, and yet there is room. And the lord said unto the servant, Go out into the highways and hedges, and compel them to come in, that my house may be filled. For I say unto you, That none of those men which were bidden shall taste of my supper. Luke 14:21-24

These harsh realities are merely a semblance of what we gradually encounter as we face the rude awakenings of ministry. We learn to understand Peter's anger and his occasional tendency to lie. We feel the constant insecurities of Thomas, whose doubtful warnings seem to come against every attempt we would make toward progress. We encounter the painful betrayal of our old friend, Judas Iscariot, whose twisted way of loving us never seems to stop him from killing us.

This is a fine dinner, indeed! If it weren't for the glorious splendor of the Host Himself, who would subject himself to the trauma? When we see Jesus, we can only sit in splendor and thank God that He is gracious enough to invite the impaired and the impoverished—lest the very seat in which we sit be emptied as well!

## SUPPERTIME IS COMING TO AN END

The truth of the matter is that no one prepares a meal to last forever. There is a time when we must move beyond suppertime. We must move beyond the stage in our development where we come to a ministry just to be fed, where our whole focus for coming to the table is always to receive. We must make the transition that every believer must make—some call it the transition from believership to discipleship, but I just call it the transition *from suppertime to service time.*

We don't need to leave the fellowship just because we've taken a closer look at the membership. If we do leave, we will only discover the sad fact that every ministry, regardless of its size or structure, has its own incapacities. God only opens your eyes so you can get up from the table and give someone else a turn in the seat. It is time for you to learn the art of service and move beyond the gluttony of supper.

"And supper being ended..." the Scripture says in John 13:2. I sense that in someone's life, supper has ended. You want desperately to go back to your original naiveté. You can no more do that than you can go back to believing in Santa Claus! Once your eyes have been opened, squeezing your eyelids together will not close them again!

What do you do? First, you must understand that suppertime is coming to an end. When you are being betrayed by those you trust, it is a sign that suppertime is coming to an end. When you reach the point where the hand that dips with you points an accusation against you, supper is coming to an end. When you want to stay where you are, but you've got to go where He calls, supper is over.

There is no need to hold on to the plate and spoon like a toddler who refuses to release his tray. Understand that God gave you that period of innocence in a time of need to accomplish what was necessary. But "supper being ended," He is clearing away the dishes. Supper is over! It is finished!

Jesus then rises from supper. I am afraid that most of us have never risen from supper. We are still trying to "get all we can, and can all we get." We have never risen from supper; instead, we are resting on the laurels of indifference and contentment. It reminds me of people who go to a restaurant and fellowship throughout the meal. Then, though the evening wanes, the candles collapse, and the flames flicker out, the crowd still sits around a cluttered table, oblivious to the need to move on.

I wonder if we have chattered away the age and jested away a generation. Are we still sitting around the cluttered dishes of dead programs whose crushed crumbs are not enough to feed the impoverished age in which we have been called? Shouldn't we have quit shouting long enough to rise from the table? Hold the music and turn up the lights! Even the waiter is gone home, and here we sit

141

in the same spot, rehearsing the same excuses! We need men and women who will rise from supper.

## ARISE TO DISROBE!

The Master now rises from the table in the presence of these, His guests, and begins the unnerving process of disrobing in a room where all others are clothed. I must tell you—after playing football in school and spending many hours in musty locker rooms with strangers—it is much easier to undress when others are undressing than it is to walk into an executive boardroom and unbuckle your belt and disrobe! This would be true even if that room was filled with the same men whom you work out with in the health spa. It is not who they are that matters. It is that your comfort zone is destroyed when you feel as though you are the only one who is naked.

Jesus taught a powerful lesson about ministry as He rose from supper and began to disrobe in front of men who were still clothed. Isn't our problem the fact that we don't want to be seen as the only one? The fear of being different can lock you in a vault. It can close you in a prison of disobedience because you are afraid of being alone.

We will never have real ministry until someone changes the atmosphere in our boring little conferences and conventions. Real ministry will start the moment we stop trying to impress each other and say, "Look! This is how I really look beneath my name, my reputation, or my success. This is who I really am!"

Jesus paid the price. He took the leap that few would ever dare to take. He laid aside His garments before those whom He had labored to inspire. Yet we have not followed His example. The closer we get to leaders, the more they hide! They are afraid, and understandably so. We have asked them to be God! We have asked them to be flawless! We have asked them to be more than what we could ever be, and we have imprisoned them in their callings and chained them to their giftings.

Wailing, shrieks of broken hearts, and screams of terror echo behind our stiffly starched shirts and satiny smooth dresses. The words have increased; the technology has improved; but the power of ministry will never be unleashed until those who are called to deliver it find the grace, or perhaps the mercy, that will allow them to *lay aside their garments*!

"Is He mad? Has He lost His mind?" Can you imagine what the disciples thought as Jesus changed the atmosphere of the feast by disrobing before them? How could a person of His stature stoop so low? I tell you, He never stood as tall as He did when He stooped so low to bless the men whom He had taught. Even Peter said, "Lord, not my feet only, but also my hands and my head" (Jn. 13:9).

We are still squirming and fuming over exposing, forgiving, and washing one another's feet! We need the whole of us cleansed! We have never accepted people in the Church. We take in numbers and we teach them to project an image, but we have never allowed people—real people—to find a place at our table!

143

Jesus was running out of time. He had no more time for fun and games. He ended the supper and laid aside His garments. Hear me, my friend; we too are running out of time! We have a generation before us that has not been moved by our lavish banquets or by the glamorous buildings we have built.

Someone, quick! Call the supper to an end and tell us who you really are beneath your churchy look and your pious posture. Tell us something that makes us comfortable with our own nudity. We have carefully hidden our struggles and paraded only our victories, but the whole country is falling asleep at the parade!

## STRIPPED DOWN TO THE ETERNAL

Jesus laid aside His garments. That is what ministry is all about. It requires you to lay aside your garments. Lay aside your personal ambitions and visions of grandeur. Gifted people tend to be some of the most egotistical, self-aggrandizing, eccentric individuals the world has ever seen. That is why "being gifted" in itself will never deliver anybody. Ministry is birthed when you are stripped down to your heart's desire, when beneath every other thread of whimsical grandeur, something in your heart says more than anything else, *I want my life to have counted for something. I want to accomplish something for God.*

Have you ever prayed the kind of prayer that pleads, "Oh God, don't let me impress anyone else but the One to whom I gave my life"?

Have we given our lives to the Lord? I am absolute-ly serious—I'm talking to those of us who witness and work in the Kingdom trying to bring souls to God. Have we given our lives to the God we teach about? If we have, then why are we still standing around the table arguing over who is going to sit on the left and who is going to sit on the right?! *Why have we not laid aside our garments?*

The garment represents different things to different people. It is whatever camouflages our realness, whatev-er hinders us from really affecting our environment. Our garments are the personal agendas that we have set for ourselves (many of which God was never consulted about). Like the fig leaves sewn together in the garden, we have contrived our own coverings. The terrible tragedy of it all is that, sooner or later, whatever we have sown together will ultimately be stripped away.

The Lord often uses trials to realign us. The strong winds of adversity will attack everything in us that can be shaken. Weaned by the wind, we release every idol in His presence. Every person who finds real purpose will, soon-er or later, go through some series of adversities that will cause them to let go of the temporal and cleave to the eter-nal. Some awaken in hospital rooms with respirators and monitors beeping in their ears. There, beneath the quiet canopy of painted ceilings and with the soft smell of dis-infectant, they realize that many of the things that seemed important mean nothing at all.

Left with nothing of importance but the simplicity of a second chance, they lay there. Their certificates of deposit in the bank, their cars in the garage, and their clothes somewhere in a closet, have all lost their importance. Beneath those thin, frail hospital sheets, they discover they are really no different from "Joe Poor" down the hall, who is there on his Medicaid card. They are stripped beneath the sheets and, for the first time, they don't care to read the paper, check the stocks, or catch the news. At least for a while, they are *naked and not ashamed*!

Others discover in the heated battle of a divorce court that the person they thought was everything can walk away and leave them for anything. With hot tears and strong angry words, they are stripped down to what they had before. Job discusses this terrible stripping that seems to be characteristic of the call. He goes through a brief but painful period that yanks away everything that appeared to be important in his life. He used to be very successful, but now he is naked and sick. His home is in shambles, his marriage is a joke, and his children—his precious children—are dead.

What word of wisdom falls from his encrusted lips? What grain of comfort does he afford himself in the vanity of his own thoughts? His only shade beneath the blistering sun of adverse circumstances is found in the fact that he can only be stripped down to what he started with before. He can be stripped of the temporal, but not the eternal.

Some things you never have to lose. I'm not talking about friends, wealth, or fame. We often forget that all of these things are mere threads and imitations of life, just shallow images of status. Character, class, and

Christianity are at least three things that can survive the strippings of life!

> *Then Job arose, and rent his mantle, and shaved his head, and fell down upon the ground, and worshipped, and said, Naked came I out of my mother's womb, and naked shall I return thither: the Lord gave, and the Lord hath taken away; blessed be the name of the Lord. In all this Job sinned not, nor charged God foolishly.* Job 1:20-22

## THE WORSHIP OF SACRIFICE

True worship is born when true sacrifice occurs. When we lay upon the altar some bleeding object that we thought we would keep for ourselves (but realized it was God's all the while), that's worship. You can never be really anointed until you personally experience a situation that calls you to lay aside your garments. It is from this river that the tears of worship are born. They fall lavishly down a face that has been pulled from behind its covering and laid bare before God. Who can help but worship Him, once we see Him aside from every distraction and weight?

People who see you worship will never be able to determine why you worship by looking at things you have. It is *what you left behind* and *laid aside* that seasons you into the real aroma of worship. How much does it cost to be the "real" you? What did you lay aside to follow Him? Whatever you have laid aside, or will lay aside, determines the effectiveness of your ability to touch the world at its feet and speak to its heart!

## Lay Aside Your Garments

Jesus, in one final blaze of teaching excellence, did an illustrated sermon in the nude. He showed the disciples that they can never change the atmosphere or wash the feet of anybody until they had gone through sacrifice and endured risk and rejection. Do you have great ambitions or plans? Lay them aside—the Lord has need of you.

Laying aside your garment requires you to say:

"Here are my grudges and my unforgiveness. Here is my need to impress and be acknowledged. Here's my time, and here is my overtime. Here's my second job. Here is anything that I may be wrapped up in that hinders me from receiving new glory.

"You will never have to take these things, Lord. You will not have to snatch them from my clenched fist as I wrestle in rebellion with Your tender whispers in the night. I have heard the soft brush of Your voice like wind across my face. I will give You what it takes to be who You want me to be. Even if I have to be *the only one* who stands in crowds of religious indifference, I will lay aside my garments!"

Jesus did the same thing in the garden of Gethsemane that He did at the end of the supper. At the supper,

He laid aside His garments; in the garden, He laid aside His will!

Thank God for all the Kathryn Kuhlmans, the Oral Roberts, and the Benny Hinns whose lives have touched the world. The hot blaze of camera lights never caught the true basis of their ministry. It was the things they *laid aside* that made them who they were. Thank God they laid them aside. Thousands are healed because they did. Thousands were saved because they did.

What about "Pastor Littlechurch" and "Evangelist Nobody" who never sold a tape or wrote a book? They paid the price nonetheless, and for the souls they touched they are unsung heroes. Like Noah, their membership roll never exceeded eight souls, but they faithfully led them nonetheless. They wanted to do more. They thought they would go farther than they did, but they had *laid aside their garments*. They said, "If I am not called to help everybody, then please, God, *let me help somebody!*" This is the cost of Christianity stripped down to one desire, stripped to the simplicity of bareness.

The truth of the matter is that when men are stripped bare, there is no difference between the executive and the janitor. When they are stripped bare, there is no difference between the usher and the pastor. Is that why we are afraid to let anyone see who we really are? Have we become so addicted to our distinctions that we have lost our commonality?

Come down from the lofty perches of superiority and wash the feet of the hurting. There are no differences in the feet of the washed and the feet of the one who washes them. They all look the same. Your ministry truly becomes effective when you know that there is precious little difference between the people you serve and yourself. Then and only then have you laid aside your garments!

This message will save a ministry. It will also save a marriage. Marriages are failing all over the country because couples are reciting vows before an overworked preacher, and an overspent family, promising to do what they will never be able to do! Why? You can't love anybody like that until you *lay aside your garments* and allow their needs to supercede your needs. Somewhere in the night, beneath the crumpled sheets of consummation, they will act out with their bodies what must happen in their hearts. They can never be one until they have laid aside their garments. Then and only then can they come together as one. There actually are people who have been married for years who have never laid aside their garments.

## OUR EXAMPLE: JESUS IN A TOWEL

Jesus so loved those men that He didn't wait on them to make the first move. He taught them by going first. He rose up! He laid aside His garments and He washed their feet! He didn't respond to their actions—He initiated their actions. Are you always going to be a responder who only reacts to what others dictate, or are you going to initiate change in the Body? If you are going to change it, then you must be willing to be a trendsetter! You must be *naked and not ashamed*.

Now I know some wise theologian is thinking, "Jesus served with a towel gird about Himself." Yes, you are right. No one can work without covering! But please remember that somewhere between His evening dinner wear and the servant's towel with which He was to be girded—somewhere in the process—Jesus stood before them naked. They witnessed the scene as their Master stepped down to become a servant. He laid aside His garments—not only for them, but for us all. He came to earth and stripped Himself of the glory He had with the Father before the foundations of the world!

> *For ye know the grace of our Lord Jesus Christ, that, though He was rich, yet for your sakes He became poor, that ye through His poverty might be rich.* 2 Corinthians 8:9

Jesus normally dressed with distinction. He was such a fashion statement that even while He was dying on the cross, affluent Roman soldiers were gambling to win the prize of Jesus' seamless robe. But this was not a time for form. Neither was it a time for fashion, for real ministry is done with a complete loss of distinction. If He were to leave a lasting impact on these men in the upper room, He must cover Himself only in a plain towel!

The glamorous Prince of Peace stripped Himself to appear before them in only a common towel. As He knelt down on the floor and began to wash the disciples' feet, He looked so lowly that it was embarrassing. Peter almost refused to allow Him to be seen in that light! To think that the One he called Master would appear in a towel! One

moment He was as stately as a prince, and the next
moment He knelt naked before them as just a man!

The final touch of God was delivered through a Man
who had humbled Himself and wrapped His vulnerabili-
ties up in His ministry. He was covered like a servant,
ready to help the hurting. His suit, His clerical attire, was
neither His seamless robe nor His nakedness. His ministry was best seen when He wrapped Himself in a towel!

> *Let this mind be in you, which was also in*
> *Christ Jesus: who, being in the form of God,*
> *thought it not robbery to be equal with God:*
> *but made Himself of no reputation, and took*
> *upon Him the form of a servant, and was made*
> *in the likeness of men: and being found in fash-*
> *ion as a man, He humbled Himself, and*
> *became obedient unto death, even the death of*
> *the cross. Wherefore God also hath highly*
> *exalted Him, and given Him a name which is*
> *above every name.* Philippians 2:5-9

If you believe that God would exalt you, if you
believe that you have the ability to wash the dusty sands
of life from the feet of this world, then please don't join
the spiritual elitists who are impressed with their own
speech!

Lay aside every distraction. Lay aside your garments, wrap every naked human flaw in the warm towel
of servanthood as you help others, and draw the water!
With joy we draw water from the wells of salvation! (See
Isaiah 12:3.) But what good is that water if we fail to use

it to wash away the weariness of someone's journey? I can almost hear the cascading sound of the cooling waters. They fall like mountains of water plummeting from the Rock. God has enough water. He just needs someone who will take the risk of being the first one. He is searching for someone to end the long supper and lay aside his garments. You may be the only one at your table who knows that the hour has come and the supper is ended. Wait no longer—we are losing our generation! *Lay aside your garments!* The waters are drawn, my friend; we are waiting...on you!

# *C*hapter 11

## STRIPPED FOR PRAYER

It is late in the evening. The sufferer walks the floor with his passion, his goals, and his ambitions. Silence envelops the house like a warm blanket around cold feet. There is a gentle caress of tranquillity holding the house in an interlude of submissive bliss. The solace of the evening has crept onto the faces of the sleeping family, softly illuminated by the moon's quiet beams.

While others sleep, there are those of us who walk the floor as a mother with a suckling child. While others enter into the bliss of calmness and lie in the warmth of peaceful beds, there are those who have a conversation where there are no ears to hear. There are those who find no solace in ordinary things in the middle of the night. They have a restlessness, almost an anticipation, that something is about to happen.

Rising like spoke from a chimney, thoughts float and ascend into the conscious mind with all the grace of a ballerina. Who can log the moment when thought becomes prayer? Sometimes it changes in the middle of a sentence. In the stillness of the night, these nightwalkers move across their rooms and stare blankly out of their windows into the dark nothingness of night. They look at something beyond vision. They speak the inaudible to the Intangible, birthing a prayer—fleeting vaporous thoughts whose pattern defies grammar. Oratorical nightmares, they are just the feeble cries of a heart whose conflict has pushed the head to bow in humble submission to One greater than itself.

## FOR GOD'S EARS ALONE

Understand that real prayer was not made for human ears. If you have a problem that can be easily prayed through in public, then it is not a problem. When we earnestly pray, we are surprised at how inner feelings we didn't even know we had come to the surface. In that regard, prayer is a nausea of the mind. It brings up the unresolved past that swirls around and around inside us.

Who of us would want others to hear us as we release our inner groanings before the throne? Religion and its images do not relieve the heart of its brokenness. There is much more involved here than the pious sputterings of religious refinement. This is a midnight cry for divine assistance! Often what we convey around others is more like a plastic-covered superficial replica of what real prayer is all about. It is a dressed-up, Sunday-go-to-meeting counterfeit that is impressive, but completely inconsequential!

## THE CHURCH'S ADVANCEMENTS

Heaven sees the hands that tightly clasp their nice gleaming Bibles in leather cases. Heaven sees the 14-karat gold necklaces draped carefully across the napes of necks held high in the glistening sunlight on Sunday morning. Only Heaven can see the liturgical order of pious hearts whose heads have contrived a method that seems spiritually edifying. The grandstands of Heaven behold the attempts of the righteous at piety and honor. How impressive are our sanctuaries—each more glamorous than the other. How stately are the auditoriums and how distinguished are the people who rush in to fill them for a punctual hour of spiritual rhetoric!

There is nothing quite comparable to the pomp and circumstance of a well-orchestrated service. Never before in the history of the New Testament Church has there been such an emphasis placed on facilities and sanctuaries. As glamorous as the old Catholic churches were in earlier years, they can't even compare to these space age monuments, these brass and glass superstructures as picturesque as the rocky crest of mountain ridges. Our jet-set, microwave age has produced some elaborate and intricately designed places of worship. We have manned them with people displaying the finest of administrative, musical, and oratorical abilities. Our cabinets are filled with resumés, statistics, and ledgers. We have arrived!

Please don't misunderstand me. I am neither commending nor criticizing these advances. My purpose is to point out the inconsistency that blares in my heart like a trumpet. I have heard the swelling tones of well-orchestrated, carefully implemented musical and theatrical presentations. However, I am often distracted by the bleating of the sheep.

Can you hear the hollow moans of sheep who bleed behind the stained glass and upon the padded pew? I do not blame our success as the cause for their pain; neither do I suggest that the absence of ornateness would cure the ills of our society. I can't help but wonder, though, if we have majored on the minor and consequently minored on the major!

## PRAYER IS...

Now understand, *nothing fuels prayer like need.* Neither the tranquil mood of a calming organ nor a dimly lit room with hallowed walls can promote the power of prayer like the aching of a heart that says, "I need Thee every hour." The presence of need will produce the power of prayer. Even the agnostic will make a feeble attempt at prayer in the crisis of a moment. The alcoholic who staggers toward a car he knows he shouldn't drive will, before the night is over, find himself attempting to dial the number of Heaven and sputter in slurred speech a fleeting prayer in the presence of near-mishap and malady.

Prayer is man's confession, "I do not have it all." Prayer is man admitting to himself that, in spite of his architectural designs and his scientific accomplishments, he needs a higher power. Prayer is the humbling experience of the most arrogant mind confessing, "There are still some things I cannot resolve."

The presence of prayer is, in itself, the birthplace of praise. Prayer is man acknowledging the sovereign authority of a God "who can!" You ask, "Can what?" God can do whatever He wants to do, whenever He wants to do it. What a subliminal solace to know the sovereignty of God!

## KEEP PERSEVERING

If there is a tragedy to this declaration, if there is any truth that numbs the glimmering joy of this theological presentation, it is that we *live among men who have replaced creations for the Creator*. Their brilliant minds grasp facts, but fail to perceive truth. The truth is not clearly seen in the facts, for the facts can suggest that you have arrived, while the truth says you are still searching! Until men come to truth, they will escape the thing that humbles the heart and bends the will to the posture of prayer.

> *And unto the angel of the church of the Laodiceans write; These things saith the Amen, the faithful and true witness, the beginning of the creation of God; I know thy works, that thou art neither cold nor hot: I would thou wert cold or hot. So then because thou art luke-warm, and neither cold nor hot, I will spue thee out of My mouth. Because thou sayest, I am rich, and increased with goods, and have need of nothing; and knowest not that thou art wretched, and miserable, and poor, and blind, and naked: I counsel thee to buy of Me gold tried in the fire, that thou mayest be rich; and*

159

*white raiment, that thou mayest be clothed,
and that the shame of thy nakedness do not
appear; and anoint thine eyes with eyesalve,
that thou mayest see. As many as I love, I
rebuke and chasten: be zealous therefore, and
repent.* Revelation 3:14-19

Each of us must have the curiosity and the inner thirst to move beyond our images into our realities. It is difficult, sometimes even painful, to face the truth about our circumstances and then possess the courage to ask for *God's best* for our lives. If prayer is to be meaningful, it cannot be fictitious. It must be born out of the pantings of a heart that can admit its need. If we refrain from airing our particular dilemmas with anyone else, at least we must be honest enough to come before God with an open heart and a willing mind to receive the "whatsoevers" that He promised to the "whosoevers" in His Word!

## BE OPEN IN TRIAL

Wrapped in the sanctity of what we profess, we often hide the nudity of what we possess. In short, we can easily find ourselves professing much more than we honestly possess. Nothing disrobes us as effectively as a trial, though. It exposes what is still lacking in our hearts and character! Although we appear to be in control in the spectators' eyes, we are often in great turmoil inside.

You would be surprised at the people who miss wonderful opportunities for God's blessing because they have "an image to uphold." They miss God's blessing because they lack the humility to assume a posture of receiving and accept God's gift through other men. Spiritual arrogance will not allow them to open their hearts to the flawed vessels that God uses. They insist on being "beyond ministry." Yet, my friend, there is a trial whose sting is as painful as the thousand darts in a beehive and as deadly as the venom of a viper.

When trials come in extreme intensity, you must adapt and be able to open your heart. Not only must we be open to the Lord, but we also must learn to be available to receive from whomever He chooses to use.

## RECEIVE FROM THE UNEXPECTED AND THE ORDINARY

I remember reading in the Gospels how Jesus needed ministry after being savagely attacked by the enemy at a very vulnerable moment. After 40 days of fasting, He was hungry (see Mt. 4:2; Lk. 4:2). Satan makes his attack when you are hungry. Hunger is a *legitimate need* that satan offers to satisfy in a perverted way. The extreme test of faith is to stand fast when you have a legitimate need you could satisfy in an illegitimate way.

The added danger of that scenario is the victim's feeling of being justified in using illicit methods because he has a *legitimate* need! Have you ever had a nagging, gnawing need that seemed to haunt you like a ghost? It taints your success and taunts your goals. It is this wrestling, this period of agonizing struggle, that teaches us how to receive ministry.

Christ seemed to have no problem rebuking the enemy who came against Him. It was after the victory was won that He needed the ministry of angels to continue His vision. There are some people who have not been released from old trials yet because they will not allow God to heal them through the angels of ministry He has chosen to use. Some have been through so much that they simply don't trust anymore. They need *someone*, but they don't trust *anyone*.

> *And He was there in the wilderness forty days,*
> *tempted of Satan; and was with the wild*
> *beasts; and the angels ministered unto Him.*
> Mark 1:13

What impresses me the most is that in order for Christ to receive the ministry of angels, He had to allow the lesser (the angels) to minister to the greater (the Christ). He allowed the angels whom He created, the same angels He commanded as Captain of the host, to minister to Him. My friend, when pain peaks, you don't care who God uses! You just want to be healed and blessed. If you were in an automobile accident and you needed help, you wouldn't care who the paramedics were. Their education, denomination, or ethnic background would mean nothing to you because of the enormity of your need.

Whenever we seek His will, we must be prepared to receive His way! Many times it is not the will of God that causes us to struggle as much as it is the *way* in which He accomplishes His will. However, if the winds beat fiercely enough and if the rains plummet down with enough thunderous force, then we are stripped by the struggle and brought to a place of open, naked prayer.

I realize that the average person can't relate to this word. But this is not a message for the ordinary. This is a message for the super-ordinary person who knows there are some trials that peel away inhibition like the rind from an orange. If you ever visit someone in the hospital and they are sitting up in bed wearing a cute gown with their hair curled, then you know they are either well cared for or they are not that sick!

## A PLACE OF NAKED PRAYER

There is a level of sickness where a suffering victim's hospital gown rides up on her body. Her hair has fallen down, and her body emits an odor. This patient knows there is someone in the room, but she just doesn't care anymore.

We need to get to the point where we lose our self-consciousness because we are sick and tired of allowing the enemy to subdue what God has given to us. We need to get to the point where *all we want is to get well*, the point where "getting well" is the only thing that really matters. Why? Stripped down somewhere below our image and our name, even beyond the opinions of others, there is a power that boggles the mind. It may just be that you can't get what you need from the Lord because you are too cognizant of people and too oblivious to the presence of God.

There is a place of *naked prayer* that we occasionally read about in the Word of God. Hannah came to the Lord in the temple and poured out her bitterness before the Lord (see 1 Sam. 1:12-18). There was so much locked up in her that when she began to empty herself out, she appeared drunk—even to the aristocracy of the church. God is raising up some people who will even blow the minds of religious people!

Radical Christians are coming to the forefront. These people have nothing to lose. Like Christ, they have been stripped on the cross and are speaking the truth under the threat of nails and spears. When we pray, we can commend not only our spirit, but also our job, home, family, finances, and everything else to the Father. We have been stripped! "Let anyone gamble for my clothes who wants them! I have learned the power of transparency and the strength of being backed in a corner."

Besides all this, we learn faith when our options diminish. Who needs faith for water anymore? We just go to the tap and get a drink. Who needs faith for the parting of the sea when there are bridges standing strong and erect? Faith is reserved for those times when there are no options, when "push" has collided with "shove"! There is nothing we can do but be crushed by the inevitable—or look unto the Invisible to do the impossible! Your crisis is a privilege because God has given you an opportunity to experience a deeper realm of miracle-working power!

## DON'T STOP NOW!

If you are going through a test and all your options are closing in without any way out, then you should get up and start shouting! *You have been chosen for a miracle.* Faith must have the incubator of impossibility to exhibit its illustrious ability. In other words, don't panic. It's just a test! However, it is a test with a reward. So don't stop short of the prize. The greater the conflict is, the greater the conquest! After all, there is a certain tightness needed to cause faith to be secreted. You can't even get toothpaste out of a tube without a firm squeeze. There is something good in you, and God knows how to get it out.

Now the pressure is mounting. The devil wants you to cry "Uncle!" He is squeezing you every way he can, but he is a liar. Let's discard what we don't need so we can activate what we do need.

Let us lay aside every sin that would so easily beset us. Now that we took that off, let's forgive everyone who ever hurt us or disappointed us. Let's just dismiss it. That's right—*throw the case out of court.* There is to be no more deliberating over the acts of men. We are about to see an act of God!

Slip the spirit of heaviness off your shoulders. That old depression is weighing you down! But don't put on the garment of praise just yet. That is what is wrong today—we have more shouters than we do prayers. Save the garment of praise, though; you're going to need it soon. Now that you are stripped to nothing but prayer, let your request be made known unto God.

I know this is radical, but you may have to walk the floor and pray. You may have to confess some issues that you have not wanted to confront, but this is *naked prayer*. You may have to forgive someone who didn't even do you the courtesy of asking to be forgiven! Do it anyway. Considering what God has done for you, you can't afford to have anything in your way.

Let the cool waters of His Word rinse the residue from your past. The Word is cascading down upon you in torrents. Spread before Him every issue. He can't cleanse what you will not expose. Bathe your mind in the streams of His mercy. There is no need to put on the "helmet of salvation" over the confusion of rejection. This kind of bathing is as holy as a christening and as refreshing as a shower.

This kind of renewal can only occur in the heart of someone who has been through enough to open his heart, to close up his past, to stand in the rain of His grace, and to tell the next generation the truth. Tell them that the only way you can dress up for God is to lay before Him as a naked offering, a living sacrifice offered up at the altar in *naked prayer*!

Additional copies of this book and other book titles from DESTINY IMAGE are available at your local bookstore.

For a complete list of our titles, visit us at www.destinyimage.com Send a request for a catalog to:

## Destiny Image® Publishers, Inc.

P.O. Box 310
Shippensburg, PA 17257-0310

*"Speaking to the Purposes of God for This Generation and for the Generations to Come"*